Stroke-Saving for the Handicap Golfer

Introduced by Peter Alliss

CRAIG SHANKLAND
DALE SHANKLAND
DOM LUPO
ROY BENJAMIN

A Sports Illustrated Book

W. Foulsham & Co. Ltd.
London
New York   Toronto   Cape Town   Sydney

FIRST EDITION
1979

ISBN 0-572-01060-5

This Sports Illustrated Book
is published by
W. Foulsham & Company,
Yeovil Road, Slough,
Berks, England,
in association with
Sports Illustrated Magazine
and
Little, Brown and Company

Designed by Susan Windheim
Published in cooperation with The Benjamin Company

Printed in Great Britain by
Lowe & Brydon (Printers) Ltd, Thetford, Norfolk

Contents

Stroke-Saving
for the Handicap Golfer

Introduction

By Peter Alliss

This book begins where most of the others leave off, and is without doubt one of the most interesting and constructive golf books to emerge for many years. It tackles clearly and positively many of golf's great taboos and mysteries and is a major addition to any golfer's library.

A good golf instruction book should contain something of value for *all* golfers, regardless of sex or standard. It should be simply explained, visually explicit and give the reader so clear an understanding of the game's mysteries that he or she can face any situation on the course with confidence. Such books are rare, but this is one of them.

It was conceived by editor and publisher Roy Benjamin as a review handbook that would provide practical answers in easy reference form to the dozens of challenges we meet each time we play. He wanted also to capture that special rapport that comes from a session on the lesson tee with a wise and understanding professional. He has succeeded in a quite unique way.

By creating a foursome which might loosely be described as teacher-writer-illustrator-amateur, he has bridged an important gap in presenting instruction for all levels of ability. Each expert knows the problems and capabilities of the average reader because each, in one way or another, identifies with what the weekender is trying to accomplish on the course.

The graphics by leading illustrator Dom Lupo, do more than interpret the golf swing: his various stop-action techniques enable the reader to *feel* the way to make a good golf shot. And accompanying the wise words and clear explanation of golfing brothers Craig and Dale Shankland, is the pungent commentary from Benjamin himself, speaking as one weekender to another.

Sound technique is paramount in golf but the majority of golfers are less concerned with striking the ball well than with scoring well. The trick is to find the balance between thorough teaching and the 'winning short cut'. This book succeeds brilliantly.

Peter Alliss

Preface

By The Ever-Hopeful Amateur (Roy Benjamin)

At the outset, let's presume that you and I have a great deal in common. We are both hopeful golfing amateurs with limited time to play or practice, and we strive for two obvious goals:

(1) We want to lower our golf scores.
(2) We want to achieve confidence and control over shots and situations we now fear or flub.

Those words represent the essence of this book's concerns.

The aim, concept, and format of this guide to better golf are totally different from any other golf book we, the authors, have ever seen — and we've seen and studied hundreds in the course of the years it has taken us to produce this book.

First of all, we are a *foursome* — working for you, plotting for you, aching for you, thinking of *you* and *your* problems — a foursome that might be loosely identified as teacher-writer-illustrator-amateur. Each of us knows your problems and your capabilities because each of us, in one way or another, identifies with what you are trying to accomplish on the golf course. Before elaborating, let me introduce the authors:

● *The teacher — Craig Shankland.* He's "The Source." Son of one of England's greatest teaching pros — Bill Shankland, a former Ryder Cup player —

Craig is a dedicated, articulate, incisive teacher whose thousands of pupils swear by him and his crystal-clear lessons. He is now the head teaching professional at the Fairview Country Club in Greenwich, Connecticut. For two years president of the New York Metropolitan Professional Golf Association and twice Pro of the Year in that PGA district, Craig knows how to explain and demonstrate golf clearly and simply. He has been on tour, has won the New York Metropolitan PGA championship, was ranked among the "top ten" club professionals for five successive years, and has played in numerous international competitions. (The "here's how" illustrations throughout the book show Craig in action as he wants *you* to be in action.)

● *The writer — Dale Shankland.* Craig's brother Dale knows the game from your point of view because of his years of experience as golf-instruction editor for *Golf Magazine.* Author-collaborator with Johnny Miller on his golf book and a teaching pro himself, Dale has the same knack as his brother for using words, symbols, and images to help you make the golf shots you want, need, and aspire to achieve.

● *The illustrator — Dom Lupo.* He is acknowledged as one of the finest and most understanding graphic interpreters of the golf swing, an expert whose various stop-action techniques help you see and feel the way to make a good golf shot. Dom is a veteran illustrator of hundreds of golf magazine features and numerous books. Many of his paintings hang in the Golf Hall of Fame at Pinehurst, North Carolina.

● *The amateur — Roy Benjamin.* As a weekend player who has enjoyed the game and wrestled with its challenges for more years than I'll admit, I probably face the same curiosities and frustrations about golf that you do. Having begun at the age of ten caddying and playing in my native Florida, I have had certain head-start advantages that have helped to make me a low-handicap player, an occasional (though not-too-successful) competitor in state, district, and country amateur tournaments, and a twelve-time winner of my own club championship at the Fairview Country Club. But, like most of you, I still turn to books and lessons and extemporaneous on-the-course (hell, sometimes *mid-swing!*) tests and experiments to try to make corrections, add distance, and solve trouble shots.

This book answers many questions we both ask, and no doubt the illustrations and suggestions will help you, as they have helped me. This is a book for *all* golfers. Even if you have played the game for years and have successfully met many of its challenges, you should be able to find in these pages tips, hints, and scraps of advice that will help you achieve that simple but elusive pair of delights — a lower score and the ability to execute one or more shots as you really want them executed.

The number of newly conquered shots and solved situations you can expect to add to your golfing arsenal by reading and applying — and *rereading* and *reapplying* — the lessons from these pages will depend on how conscientious you are, and on how far from perfect you estimate your game to be. Inasmuch as *no* golfer — whether tour superstar, teaching pro, or scratch amateur — can claim the unattainable state of perfection, it stands to reason that the need to find solutions to golfing problems will always exist.

Our desire to help you discover and apply the solutions to your problems motivated the four of us to pool our resources and to assemble, sort out, classify, and set down — in words and pictures — enough practical advice so that on as many occasions as possible — before, after, or during a round — you can say to yourself: "I recognized the challenge and I successfully met it."

Like many amateur golfers, I have experienced the frustrations that come from trying to imitate the playing style of superstars who have written books outlining their personal techniques. "Swing as I do" is the theme of most of these manuals. But only a fortunate few of us part-time golfers have the ability to "follow the stars." Being a book publisher by profession and a golfer by addiction, I had for years searched for a book that would: (1) be the next-best thing to a lesson session on the tee with a wise and understanding teaching professional; and (2) serve as a brushup or review handbook that would provide (away from the golf course, for pre-game and postgame study) practical answers, in easy-reference form, to the dozens of challenges we meet in every round of golf we play. No luck in my search — but there may be an answer here. By outlining and developing this new book, in association with my three talented partners, I hope my dual goal has been achieved.

This instruction book focuses the experience and know-how of Craig Shankland, a unique *teaching* professional whose thousands of hours on the lesson tee gives him a keen and sympathetic understanding of the amateur's frailties and limitations; Craig Shankland is the kind of teacher who can articulate advice that you can easily and successfully follow. Furthermore, our authoring team has responded to the kinds of questions you are most likely to ask a golf professional on the practice tee or during a playing lesson.

What are the questions and problems most likely to concern you and me? Adhering to the basics and knowing what goes into making a good shot are obvious fundamentals of learning. That's only the beginning, though. Curing bad shots, conquering trouble shots, executing challenge shots and recovery shots — those are the subtle extras you will find covered in this book. (And to make your search for the answers easier, the contents page conveniently classifies most of the situations that are now likely to concern or baffle you.)

As one amateur to another — and as a collaborator with our teacher, Craig Shankland, on this book — I have briefly introduced each of the seven chapters with my reactions to Craig's instructions. You will find my remarks in italic type, preceded by the caption *Amateur's Note.*

When you analyze golf, you realize that its greatest pleasures are derived from two diametrically opposed situations. One is the positive side, where you execute basics to achieve preplanned results. (We call these the shots that "warm your heart.") The other is the negative side, where the thrill results from overcoming forces that are constantly endeavoring to throw you off balance.

On the negative side, you accept — along with golf's never-monotonous, always-intriguing aspects — those obstacles without which there would be no game: wind, rough, trees, uneven terrain, bunkers, water hazards, undulating greens. You also battle pressure — "choking" and fear. How you overcome these natural, man-made, and mental difficulties ultimately dictates your success in reaching your goals — that lower score and the executed-as-planned shot.

That is why we feel that some of the most important contributions this book can make to your game are contained in chapters five and six, which deal with trouble shots, recovery shots, and challenge shots. In those two chapters you will find a conveniently categorized treatment of nearly one hundred situations that cover most of golf's challenges. Recognize them. Know that *all* who play the game face them — from the lowliest hackers to the gold-laden champions. Approach these trouble shots with confidence and a knowledge of what is required to conquer them. When you do this you'll have taken the most satisfying and rewarding steps possible toward enjoying the game and getting pride from your achievements.

Incidentally, it was the section on trouble shots that first inspired this book. Wouldn't it be valuable, we reasoned, for the reader-golfer to be able to turn to a specific problem (before or after the game) and put his or her finger on the solution to that problem? True, next week's problems may be different, and what you read this week may not be so happily executed next week; but many of your answers do lie in this section.

So skip, jump, search out *your particular momentary needs* in chapters five and six. Don't be afraid to refer again and again to the same bothersome situation. It's no secret that the muscles are not always willing servants of the mind. We won't promise that you'll truly conquer *every* trouble shot. But we'll help you try, because we understand your plight and appreciate your desire to master the game's difficult situations. Examples:

● *Buried lie in a trap near the green.* Many golfers cringe, groan, and curse the fates that give them the "fried-egg lie" in the sand (where the top of the ball is barely visible). That shot — inevitably a "trouble" shot — is just as much a part of the game as setting up the ball for your drive on the first tee. There's no need to go jelly-kneed at the challenge. You *can* extricate yourself and you *can* get close enough to the pin for a one-putt opportunity. (To find out how, turn to chapter five, page 112, "The Buried Lie.")

● *An intentional hook to curl around a tree and reach a green.* The pros do it for you on TV and you marvel at their mysterious abilities. You can do it too. Take this likely situation: You are in the rough and there is a tree between you and the green. Discretion may often call for a safe shot to the fairway. Ah, but in match play — or with a pound note riding — what may be required is an intentional hook to avoid the tree and draw neatly to the green. Luck or misguided hopes are not the answer. And you *can* execute the shot. (Turn to chapter six, page 167, "The Intentional Hook.")

● *Driving into a strong, head-on wind.* This shot baffles, frustrates, and even angers many a golfer, who often finds that the mightier the effort, the punier the result. But there are sound and simple suggestions that will produce very satisfactory results. (Turn to chapter five, page 140, "Hitting Against the Wind.")

Let's face it: golf enthusiasts are too often looking for easy answers when they put their money on the line and buy a golf book. They seem to hope for an impossibility: *The* Secret, The All-Purpose Gimmick, The Mystery "X" Factor, The Fad-of-the-Moment, The Holy Grail, The Shortcut, The Instant Answer, The Painless Solution. They sometimes forget that the complexities, challenges, and variables in golf are what make it the most intriguing game ever contrived.

Our challenge in this book is to present solid,

practical, workable, understandable, and *applicable* instruction. To read a tip and understand it is only the first step; to apply it, as you play, is the acid test.

The nongolfer cannot comprehend the game's bittersweet allure. There is the agony of shanking a simple approach into a trap guarding the green, when winning the match required only that you hit the green and get down in two putts. There is also the ecstasy (particularly when the lie in the trap is a buried one) of recovering from that gaffe with a properly executed, confidently swung, closed-face sand shot that ends up three feet from the hole — enabling you, after all, to execute the winning one-putt stroke.

Good luck, fellow golfers. Welcome to the world of lower scores, achieved because you knew what you were supposed to do . . . and you did it!

1

A Quick Review of the Basics

Amateur's Note

"The grip and the alignment are the foundations of the golf swing!"

That is Craig's undying theme song. The grip is what he first inspects when a player gets on the practice tee for a lesson. In the next few pages, Craig relates your grip to good and bad shots. (Incidentally, unless otherwise indicated, all the discussion, instruction, examples, and illustrations that follow assume a right-handed golfer — left-handers should "transpose" and execute accordingly.)

Remember this basic truth: Whenever you develop a disappointing and erratic pattern in your shots, refer first to your grip before applying any other suggested changes.

Also, check your alignment, setup, and position in relation to the ball. You will see later in this book important references to visualization and feel for the shot you are about to make. But seeing the shot in your mind's eye will not deliver the desired result if you have not mastered your grip and aimed yourself properly.

Your Grip

The foundation of any golf swing is the grip. Only if your hands are positioned correctly initially will it be possible to develop a sound, consistently reliable swing. If you start off with your hands incorrectly positioned, you'll be building your golf swing around a fault and will be forced to compensate in order to return the clubhead to the ball in a desirable square-to-the-target position. As a teacher, I have found that nearly all bad shots are the result of a bad grip.

Say, for example, that your hands are in what is termed a *strong position*, turned so far to the right on the grip of the club that the inverted V's created by your thumbs and forefingers point to the right of your right shoulder. This will cause the clubface to *close* (aim to the left) at impact and the ball will hook. To compensate, you will have to make the clubhead follow an exaggerated in-to-out path just to keep the ball in play.

Conversely, if you have a *weak grip*, where the

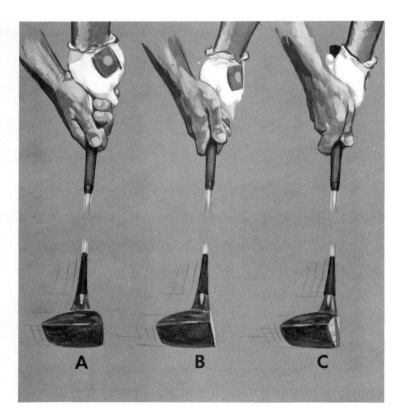

Note the marked effect the grip has on the swing For a right-handed player, if the palms are tilted to the right (A), the clubface will return to the impact area in a closed position (aimed to the left). If the palms are properly aligned (B), the hands will work correctly and return the clubface in the desirable square position. If the palms are turned to the left (C), the clubface will be returned in an open position (aimed to the right) at impact.

hands are turned to the left so that the V's point to the left shoulder, the clubface will tend to return to the ball in an *open position* (aimed to the right) and you'll slice. The compensation that you would have to make then — again, solely to keep the ball in play — would be an exaggerated out-to-in swing. Golf students who take the time to master correct positioning of their hands will be on the most direct course to improvement. Because they don't have to make compensations, they will gain a much better understanding of shot direction, and eventually will command enough control to maneuver the ball — hit it either left-to-right or right-to-left, at will.

If your grip is bad, it will be impossible for your body to function properly, because the swing is a chain reaction. The correct grip will allow your body to wind and unwind in sequence. You can't possibly play good golf with a good swing and a bad grip. However, with a good grip and a bad swing you can always improve.

POSITIONING
YOUR HANDS

The grip that I advocate to my students is the *Vardon overlapping*, in which the little finger of the right hand goes over and around the knuckle of the left forefinger. This grip has proved over the years to be the most effective union of hands and club. It molds the hands together, giving a close-knit feeling, while at the same time allowing the wrists to be used freely without loss of accuracy.

Before I show you how to position your hands on the grip of a club when you pick it up, I would like to make a point without the club. Assume a normal golf stance, as though you were going to hit the ball, feet shoulder-width apart, and let your arms hang

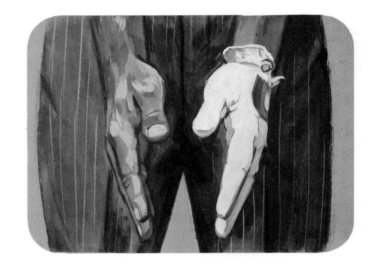

freely against your sides. Now extend your arms straight out, holding your hands at the same angle, palms facing one another. Once your arms are fully extended in front of you, note that the palms are perpendicular to the target line. This is the natural position they should be in once the grip is completed.

At the point of impact, the hands instinctively return to the "palms-facing" position. To get a better understanding of what I mean, extend your right arm in front of you and rotate the hand in a clockwise direction until the palm faces the sky. This position represents a "strong" grip. Were you to assume a "strong" grip (one with your hands turned to the right on the club), your right palm would be facing skyward initially but would return to impact facing the target; the clubface would be closed. The reverse is true if you rotate your palm to the left on the club:

Stand with your feet shoulder-width apart and your arms hanging normally by your sides, then extend both arms until the palms of your hands are perpendicular to the target.

this would represent a "weak" grip and when the palms returned to the palms-facing position, the clubface would automatically be open.

GETTING A GRIP
ON THE CLUB

To insure that both hands assume the palms-facing position, first rest the club against your belly button and let your arms hang naturally at your sides. Then move your hands up, with the palms still perpendicular to the target line, so that the grip of the club is sandwiched diagonally in between. Now just wrap your fingers around the handle. Be sure not to rotate your hands.

Your hands should be placed on the grip of the club with the palms in the perpendicular (or "palms-facing") position.

Two useful checkpoints will help you grip correctly each time: (1) see that only the knuckles of

the forefinger and middle finger are visible on the left hand, and (2) see that the inverted V's created by the thumbs and forefingers point directly at the right shoulder, not to either side of it.

Most advocates of the palms-facing grip suggest that the V's should point to the chin. While this might prove a successful position for the professional or low-handicap amateur, it is not a good position for the average golfer. The average player will derive more power and significantly more control by having the V's aimed at the right shoulder. Surprisingly, this is still a palms-facing position. Unless you consciously manipulate your hands into a "weaker" position, you'll find that the V's naturally point to your right shoulder.

It is imperative that any player strive to get to a stage where he or she can position the hands purely by *feel*, without going through a one-finger-at-a-time process. This, of course, can only be accomplished through practice; there is no shortcut.

HOW HARD SHOULD YOU SQUEEZE THE CLUB?

How much energy ought it take to hold a club that weighs around fourteen ounces? About the same amount that it would take to hold an uncooked egg. Were you to grip too hard, the egg would break. If you imagine that you have an egg in each hand when you address the ball, you will have the right amount of pressure in your grip and it will be equally distributed, which is important for a smooth takeaway. Too much pressure could cause tension to spread up into the forearms and shoulder muscles, which would seriously hinder a free-flowing swing. A tense player loses the clubhead speed vital for distance and will also lose control by tending to steer the ball. It is therefore vital to be aware of grip pressure and to eliminate tension from the address. So remember: Hold the club about as hard as you would hold an uncooked egg.

Your Alignment and Setup

Every good player has his or her own method of setting up, a method that does not vary from shot to shot. A systematic setup helps you get aligned with and tuned in on your target every time you address a golf ball. It makes your address and swing more organized and positive, and you are able to keep your mind off the negative. You'll have no time to worry about the out-of-bounds markers on the left or the trees on the right because you'll be too busy making sure that you are set up correctly. Most players coming down to the post, whether in a tournament or in a friendly match, tend to speed up. In their haste they forget the essentials, such as grip, stance, and alignment, and they forget where they are aiming the ball. To let your guard down for a second on the course is to invite disaster. Negative thoughts — images of the out-of-bounds markers, lakes, or trees — filter slowly into the mind. Don't allow this to happen. Keep your mind focused on positive action. Adopt a constant pattern when addressing the ball and in tight situations stick to it no matter what.

The pattern illustrated here, broken down into four steps, is the one I use, although I don't suggest that it is the only possible pattern of address; I offer it only as a model. If you prefer to develop your own specific pattern, fine.

1. I stand directly behind the ball and visualize the target line. Then I pick out a spot, a divot, a mark on the grass, or a broken tee — something that is directly on the intended line of flight and reasonably close to the ball. It is easier and just as accurate to line up the shot using an object close to the ball instead of the distant target.

2. I move diagonally to a point at a right angle to the ball, turn, and place the clubface down, aimed "through" the marker spot toward the target.

3. I step in with my right foot and set it a comfortable distance from the ball.

4. Then I set my left foot down parallel to the intended line of flight and also check to see that my shoulders are also parallel to the line. After two waggles I start my swing.

The full sequence is automatic, like "Get ready — Get set — Go!" — but you should follow your routine methodically, smoothly, unhurriedly.

2

The Hub — A Simple Guide to Help You Groove Your Swing

Amateur's Note

The hub is a mental image used by Craig Shankland as a simple and effective device to focus the amateur's mind on a very crucial element in executing a sound golf stroke: a grooved, consistent swing.

Craig often talks about the hub — basically the swing's center — as the best possible image to enable you to understand and to picture your own swing. (Most golfers, including topflight pros, are astounded to see their own swing in photographs. How we look and how we think we look are often totally different.)

"Put another way," Craig says, "if you are hitting bad shots — pulling, topping, or skying — you can be sure that your hub is shifting."

Why the Hub Is So Important to You

Like a large wheel, a golf swing has a center, called the *hub*. If this center were to wobble or shift, then the whole revolution, the circumference, the entire arc of the swing would be affected.

In a golf swing, the hub is principally the player's head. However, if a large enough depiction of the hub were drawn around the head, its lower half would incorporate the neck and shoulders. It is essential, then, that the head, neck, and shoulders remain perfectly centralized throughout the swing.

Other than those which result from bad grips, most bad shots occur when the hub moves from its original starting position. This excess movement can result in shanked (heeled), sclaffed, topped, fat, sliced, skied (pop up), daisy-cutter , pulled, pushed, smothered, or totally whiffed shots, depending on how the hub shifts. If the hub moves in *any* direction, the swing circumference is affected and sound contact of the clubhead with the ball becomes unlikely.

Only when the hub remains centralized can you produce consistent shots: not only can you repeat your actions, but you can feel them taking place. Repetition is the key to consistency. Being able to repeat the same movement, shot after shot, allows you the control necessary to negotiate eighteen holes on a golf course and to avoid the wild, erratic shots that occur when you are unable to repeat your swing.

In the illustrations that follow, you will see the dramatic effect that the hub has on the swing. Note that in each case when the head, neck, and shoulders, and thus the hub, moves — to the right, to the left, up, down, or toward the ball — the fault becomes compounded on the arc circumference of the wheel.

As a teacher, I can safely say that inadvertent hub movement ranks along with a bad grip as the primary fault among average golfers. Teachers, low-handicap players, and duffers alike use many names for this movement — swaying, dipping, lifting, and so forth. Yet the fact remains that all these faults have but one cause: an unsteady hub.

A good way to implant a sound hub position into your swing is to imagine that you have a tray of teacups balanced on your head. Should the hub move in any direction, the tray would topple off your head and the cups would crash around your feet. Some teachers believe that consciously keeping the head still is inhibiting. But if you have ever watched African natives walk with giant vessels on their heads, you've seen that though their heads remained perfectly still there was absolutely no restriction in their shoulders, arms, and lower body. Those vessels wouldn't stay balanced if their heads moved, would they?

I am not suggesting that a steady hub is the only answer, or the only secret, to a sound golf swing. It is, however, a prime factor in developing a good, consistent swing, as the following pages demonstrate.

The Hub on Your Backswing

Throughout your backswing the center of the *hub* — the smaller shaded area in the illustrations — should remain perfectly steady. Your shoulders should revolve around this fixed axis, while your left arm remains perfectly straight, creating an arc radius (extending from the clubhead to your shoulder), which is necessary for control and power. This radius must create the largest possible "circular" arc around the hub.

The Hub on Your
Downswing and Follow-Through

The hub should remain stationary within the arc of the swing. The body position and clubhead position at impact should almost duplicate the situation in the original address (the only difference is that your legs and hands should be slightly "ahead" of the ball laterally — closer toward target). The follow-through completes the circular arc of the swing.

Moving the Hub Up

If the hub moves upward, the lower arc of the swing moves up as well. At impact, the clubhead returns to a position above the ball; only the bottom half of the clubface makes contact. This tendency results in a topped shot or a daisy-cutter– both of which often plague the average player's game.

Moving the Hub Down

When the hub moves down during the backswing, the arc moves down with it; the clubhead is thus below the ball at impact. The result will be a fat, sclaffed, or skied shot (as described in chapter four.)

Moving the Hub Forward

If the hub moves forward, toward the ball, the club is forced to follow an unnatural arc outside of the normal path. The result: the clubhead arrives in the impact area *beyond* the ball. At impact, the neck of the club (the *hozel*) makes contact, causing a shanked (heeled) shot that goes nowhere.

Moving the Hub Right

If the hub moves to the right — away from the target — during the backswing, the rest of your body,
as well as the swing arc, will move the same way.
Unless you try to return the hub to its original
starting position by swaying back toward the target
in mid-swing, all power will be lost behind the ball.
Since swaying back to the left is a compensating
move that requires considerable effort to synchronize
correctly, the chances of solid contact are reduced.

Moving the Hub Left

When the hub moves left — toward the target — so does the circular path of the clubhead. Thus, the arc radius behind the ball is reduced drastically, and all the extension — since the body is ahead of the ball — is wasted beyond impact. Moreover, the downswing arc will be altogether too steep, causing the clubhead to arrive at the ball in a hooded position. The result will be a smothered shot.

Shift Your Weight, Not the Hub

Unless you shift your weight from right to left — toward the target — during your downswing, you will create the effect of keeping your hub too far right and the desired arc position will be lost. There will be very little extension, plus a short arc radius

at impact and follow-through — in other words, a power loss. Furthermore, the clubhead will be forced back into the impact area while moving *upward*. The result is wasted effort: a topped shot that hardly goes anywhere. Your weight must shift — for power and accuracy — but *the hub must remain steady*.

3

Good Shots That "Warm Your Heart"

Amateur's Note

Craig's "Good-Shot Philosophy" is simple but basic: Good shots result from executing fundamental swing movements correctly.

Good shots are the result of practice after good instruction, of knowing what you are doing and why you are doing it, of making your swing consistent, of executing your movements in an unhurried, smooth, and relaxed manner.

A "good shot," says Craig, "is the result of having done everything right. There is no shortcut. You can't buy good shots for any amount of money. You and only you can perform them, and during competition on the golf course, no one can guide or assist you. You alone are the master of your golfing fate."

The Long, Straight Drive

There is nothing more exhilarating than hitting a long, straight drive. It is perhaps the most rewarding experience in golf.

A straight drive off the first tee while all your friends are watching can give you an added lift and lead to your scoring a low round. And if it's a *long*, straight drive, aside from giving you a psychological advantage over your opponent, it will long be remembered around the clubhouse. Your ego will constantly be boosted by ambassadors who'll spread the word throughout the club about your "amazing" ability to hit the long ball. In the locker room after playing, you'll hear, "Did you see Don's drive off One? — must've been three hundred yards." You may in fact have scored your worst round of the season. The long drive is remembered, the bad score quickly forgotten.

To hit a long, straight drive you must be physically qualified for the experience. You must be able to make a full, relaxed turn of your body from backswing to follow-through, without restriction. The combination of turn, arc radius, timing, and tempo gives you power and control. Brute force is not the answer. You could weigh 21 stones and have arms like telephone poles, but all the force you could muster wouldn't send the ball very far at all. On the other hand, you could weigh 10 stones and hit the ball anywhere from 240 to 300 yards just by harnessing your power through timing. The secret to the long ball lies as much in control of the mind as in control of the body. You can't be overanxious if you want to get the most out of your driver.

THE DRIVER SETUP

The setup plays as much a part in securing success with the driver as the swing itself. In fact, if you aren't set up correctly the odds are against your hitting the ball well.

The ball must be positioned off your left heel. You need a wide stance, your feet slightly outside shoulder-width apart. This will place most of your body weight — especially your head, which adds a large portion of the total weight — behind the ball. Your hands and the clubface should be in line with the ball.

I recommend a *square* stance when hitting with

Position the ball off your left heel, feet just outside shoulder-width apart, hands and clubface in line with the ball.

the driver. (A "square stance" means the feet are parallel to the intended line of flight.) Any other stance, open or closed, would require you to compensate in the swing to steer the ball into the center of the fairway. With a square stance you can take a square swing and aim the ball directly at your target. With the others, if you failed to compensate you would force the ball to curve in one direction or the other.

Your left arm must be comfortably straight when addressing the ball. This does not mean rigid; flexibility is a necessity. Your left arm establishes the width of arc in the swing by remaining straight until just after the ball has been struck. All you have to do then, once you have initially established your straight left-arm extension, is turn.

THE DRIVER SWING

If your left arm was straight at address, simply turn and you'll have the needed arc radius.

Your shoulders dominate the backswing turn. Simply by turning your shoulders your arms will follow. And the extension created by the straight left arm will be maintained without conscious effort for as long as the shoulders turn. I don't believe that forcing the clubhead away from the body, by pushing it low to the ground, is necessary. If your shoulders turn around a steady head position and your left arm remains reasonably straight you'll have the necessary arc radius for power and control.

Your turn should be tension-free and relaxed. Too often a player who is scared of the driver grips tightly during the address and tension spreads to the forearms and shoulders. Tension shortens arc radius; consequently, valuable motion (turning ability) is lost. The swing becomes jerky and short, powerless and without control. Don't let this happen. You should hold the club firmly but not too tightly. Be conscious of keeping tension out of your shoulder muscles. Stay loose and complete your backswing turn (windup).

You know you are fully turned when the muscles down your left side start to stretch, when your left shoulder is under your chin, or when your back is facing the hole. Out on the course, these keys can be useful to help you complete your backswing turn.

In the ideal top-of-the-swing driver position the club is nearly horizontal, with the clubshaft pointing directly at the target. Your left knee is pointed inward, to the right of the ball, and most of your body weight is on your right foot. Your head is still centered directly over the ball. From here you're in position to start the downswing.

Whereas the backswing is dominated by the shoulders, the responsibility of the downswing and follow-through is given to the lower body, specifically the knees and hips. You initiate your downswing by shifting the weight back to your left side through a *lateral* drive (a move in the direction of the target) in your knees. This starts an unwinding sequence in your upper body. Once your weight, led by your knees, is onto the left side, your hips assume the leadership role by clearing quickly out of the way. In professional terminology this is called *separation*. If there is a secret to power and consistency with the driver, separation is it. The knee and hip actions separate the lower body from the upper and create the driving power as the wrists catapult the clubhead into and through the impact area at maximum speed. The knees initiate, then the hips follow, leading ahead of the upper body, to act as the unwinding key.

To insure that you retain clubhead speed — vital for both distance and accuracy — the clubhead on

A full turn of your shoulders is essential for a reliable swing. At the top of the backswing the clubshaft should be in nearly a horizontal position, pointing toward target.

You initiate your downswing with a lateral drive made by your knees. This shifts the weight to your left side.

The clubhead is catapulted through the impact area by the wrists. Without wrist action there can be no clubhead speed.

Unwind to face toward target, and take the clubhead as far through as you are able. At the finish your hands and the clubhead should be behind you.

follow-through should be allowed to go through as far as possible. At the finish your hands and the clubhead should be behind you, and your hips and shoulders should be facing directly at your target.

The Fairway Woods

Don't underestimate the importance of fairway woods. Gary Player, one of the greatest players in the history of the game, had serious distance problems when he first came to the United States. He was used to courses where the premium was placed on accuracy rather than distance. After a few months playing on the U.S. tour, he became frustrated by his inability to reach many of the par 5s that the American pros reached easily. So he returned to South Africa and began exercising and working hard on his game, especially his fairway woods. When he returned to the United States, Player could hit the par 5s and he began winning. Today, he is one of the best fairway wood players in the game.

Effective use of the fairway woods can do for you what it did for Player: make the long par 4s and 5s easier to cope with. If you decide to use a fairway wood, however, your choice of which one (3, 4, 5, et cetera) should not always be based on the distance to the target; consider also the type of lie you have. For example, if the ball is sitting up in lush fairway grass, you have all the options. But if it is sitting down on hard ground, unless you are an extremely capable fairway wood player, I strongly suggest you sacrifice yardage for a percentage shot and choose a more lofted wood.

As to technique, I don't recommend any drastic changes compared to the way you hit with a driver. Place the ball in line with your left heel and set your feet parallel to the target line (a square stance). Position your weight evenly between the heels and the balls of both feet. And be sure to allow the club-head to rest with its soleplate flat on the ground. The clubface should squarely face your intended target.

On the backswing, be especially conscious of making a full shoulder-turn. Many bad shots occur because players make short, quick backswings. The

With all fairway woods, make a conscious effort to watch the ball until it has been hit.

If you need more height, simply hit down more.

To gain maximum clubhead speed and control, use your hips, legs, and feet to assist in the acceleration of your arms and hands.

backswing must be full and smooth and must emphasize the shoulder-turn.

In the downswing, acceleration and a conscious effort to stay down, keeping your hub steady, will do the trick. Remember, you can't hit the ball very far using just your wrists and arms. So use your hips, legs, and feet to assist the acceleration of arms and hands for maximum clubhead speed and control.

One last word of advice: If you need additional height on the fairway wood shots, simply hit down into the ball more. The more height you need, the more you should hit down and through.

The Long Irons

To begin with, it's important to emphasize that the long irons are, compared to the rest of the clubs in the bag, a little bit harder to use because they don't have much *loft* (clubface angle) and they have longer shafts than the middle and short irons. Less loft on the clubface produces less spin on the ball, resulting in a lower trajectory. Shots hit with 5-, 6-, 7-, and 8-irons will all rise even if the ball is slightly mishit, but this isn't the case with the long irons. And because the shaft is longer, your swing's arc radius will be longer and therefore harder to control.

Though it may sound as if I'm starting off on a negative note, I'm making these points so you're aware that you can't make a haphazard swing with these clubs. But don't be afraid of long irons — the

2-, 3-, and 4-irons play a very important part in stroke-saving. They should be neither feared nor ignored.

The most common cause of bad long-iron shots is fear. Fear creates tension, which in turn leads to jerky, uncontrolled swings. So the first point I want to make with regard to technique is: relax. Your long-iron swing must be no different from any other iron swing. Don't grip too tightly, don't get tense — just relax.

To help offset the club's lack of loft and its long shaft, you should play the ball off the left heel in the address. With the ball in this position at impact, the club will not be moving down as much — the arc will be wider and more sweeping behind the ball — which will give you more height.

Other than the ball-position change (more off the left foot), most of the other fundamentals remain the same. Your weight should be evenly balanced on both feet, with your hands just slightly ahead of the ball laterally (toward target); your feet should be aligned parallel to the intended flight line. The only difference in positioning your feet for a long iron shot is that they are set slightly wider, to give you a solid base for a little bit longer swing. Now, on to the swing.

I'm asked all the time by my pupils: How should you take the club back on long-iron shots? I encourage golfers just to start the club back with the shoulders rather than worry about coordinating individual parts of the body. If the shoulders start the swing, everything else will follow naturally. The left arm will remain extended throughout the backswing for as long as the shoulders turn. If the shoulders don't turn enough on a long-iron swing, the arms and hands take over and effort is wasted. I can't empha-

I can't emphasize enough the importance of completing the shoulder-turn. Only then will the extension created by the left arm at address give you the swing arc radius necessary for success with the long irons.

Be sure that you accelerate the clubhead through to a full finish. Your hips and shoulders should be facing the target directly, your weight should be on your left side, and your hands should be high, behind your head.

size enough the importance of completing the shoulder-turn. And remember, as I said earlier, fear is a common cause of long-iron problems: it creates tension, which causes shortness in the range of motion — the distance the club is swung back. A conscious effort to relax and complete the shoulder-turn — making sure that your left shoulder arrives under your chin and that your back is to the hole at the top of the backswing — will help insure success.

Your lower body must lead the clubhead back to the ball on the downswing. If your upper body leads, you will hit the shot badly. When your lower body beats the clubhead to the ball and separates from your upper body, the clubface is prevented from closing and arrives back at the ball in a square or slightly open position — you get the trajectory that you need.

Another point on long-iron mechanics deals with the follow-through. Most high-handicap players direct too much attention at the ball when trying to achieve a high trajectory. They forget to accelerate the clubhead all the way through the swing to a full finish. The one thing you must not allow is deceleration — allowing the clubhead to slow down as it passes through the impact area. Consciously follow through to a full finish. At the end of the swing your hips and shoulders should face the target directly, your weight should be concentrated on your left side, and your right foot should be on its toe with the heel off the ground. Overall, you want to feel as if you have completed a gigantic circle, ending with the clubshaft and the clubhead behind your head and with your hands in a high position.

Finally, I want to stress the importance of good long-iron tempo and restrained force. Don't try to hit the ball any harder than you would with a middle or short iron. Swinging too hard is a major fault in most players' games. I often have my students hit five or six shots with a short iron, then hit the same number with a long iron. I consider this an excellent way of demonstrating to them that additional force is not necessary with long irons. Most golfers think that when they hit a longer, less-lofted club they must swing harder, which just is not true. The reduced loft alone will give extra distance; all that's necessary is a smooth swing. If you hit a few shots using the exercise I've just outlined, you'll see what I mean. So, when you're next faced with that crucial long-iron shot: relax, turn, start down with your lower body, and be sure to accelerate through to a full finish. And make the whole swing smooth.

The Middle Irons

The 5-, 6-, and 7-irons, also called the middle irons, are among the easiest clubs in the bag to use. Because of the amount of loft on the clubface of a middle iron it is easy to get the ball airborne. And because the middle iron's shaft is shorter than a long iron's, the clubhead arc is easier to control; there is very little chance of sending the ball too far off line.

But if you play regularly, don't make the common mistake of letting your guard down. Just because it's a middle-iron shot doesn't make it a cast-iron cinch that you'll play the shot well. There are some key points to keep in mind.

Be sure to know how far you can hit the ball with each club. A middle iron can be used effectively by the average golfer to hit a distance of anywhere from 130 to 150 yards; with the same club, a lower-handicap player might hit the ball between 140 and 170 yards.

The middle iron's greatest attribute is its effect on ball trajectory. Because of the loft on the clubface, the ball will fly high and will stop quickly when it lands. A longer-iron shot isn't quite as predictable because it will fly lower and roll more. When a pin placement is cut close to a trap you can fly the ball right at the flag with a middle iron, whereas with a long iron, from a greater distance, you would be unable to do so.

The main technique difference on a middle-iron shot is that the ball is played in the center of the stance. This is the low point of the downswing arc and the place where you'll strike the ball crisply. Your weight should be equally distributed between both feet and your stance and body must be aligned parallel to the intended line of flight.

Emphasis during the swing should be placed on tempo. Of course, the only way you can have good tempo is if you coil and uncoil your body correctly. Be conscious of completing your shoulder-turn in the backswing. It is very easy to let your guard down and shorten your swing with middle irons. Don't. Complete your turn and then be very conscious of initiating your downswing with your legs and hips. Then you'll find you unwind freely and swing smoothly down and through to a full finish.

The middle-iron ball should be played in the middle of your stance, with your weight equally divided between both feet.

The Short Irons

THE FULL-WEDGE   The short-iron swing must be full. The most common cause of bad shots with 8-irons, sand irons, and the like is thinking that a short swing is needed because such clubs have shorter shafts and considerably more loft than all the others. Your swing must be as full as if you were playing a driver. The shorter shaft and sharper loft enable you to control the height and distance you hit the ball. The mechanics for a short shot are otherwise no different from a middle-iron shot.

The best short-iron players are able to control the *speed* of the club. Instead of concentrating on how far back they take the club on the backswing and how far they follow through, they are more concerned with how much force they put into the motion. Thus they can swing with more freedom and aren't distracted by precise mechanics. The ball, after all, responds only to the speed of the clubhead through the impact area, so the player who is able to reduce or increase the speed of the overall motion depending on the distance required is able to vary the length of shots without shortening the swing. (I'm talking now, of course, in terms of full shots. When you get very close to the green, within pitching or chipping distance — which I'll cover in the next section — the swing length must be reduced.) If, for example, you normally hit your 8-iron shot 125 yards but you are faced with a shot of only 115 yards, there's no way you can swing using full force. You're going to have to slow your tempo a little or choose a shorter club. This is a matter of feel that comes from experience. You must practice.

Practice the in-between distances that you will

encounter on the course — the shots that require a little less than maximum force. Start out by hitting full shots. Record either mentally or on paper how far you hit your 8-iron, 9-iron, pitching wedge, and sand irons with your normal swing. Then, gradually, making the same full swing, slow the tempo down. With the pitching and sand wedges, go from using full force to using minimum force. You'll be surprised to find that you're able to hit the ball only a very short distance although using a full swing. Only when you can hit the ball no shorter should you elect to shorten the swing in length.

The short-iron swing must be full, with emphasis placed on good tempo. Make the same full swing regardless of the distance you want the ball to travel. To vary distance, simply regulate the amount of force you put into the total motion.

THE HALF-WEDGE

Once you are close to the green, you should cut your swing in half. You need an action in which the club-head goes only to about hip height on both back-swing and follow-through.

The swing I advocate on these shorter shots is really only a smaller version of the big swing. I'm not a believer in fancy changes, such as sharp wrist-breaks or outside-the-line swings. You've got to keep it simple. The fewer swing-thoughts you have in your mind, the easier it is to retain a perspective on the target and the distance you need to hit the ball. It's really like tossing a wad of paper into a waste-paper basket. You see the basket and you rely on your instinct and experience to provide the necessary force and accuracy to get the paper into the bin. But suppose you were conscious of even one or two movements within the throwing action — would you be able to throw as freely? Of course not. You'd clog your spontaneity.

It's the same with short shots. Your mind has to be reasonably free, not conscious of any more than one

A pitch shot is a lot like throwing a wad of paper into a wastepaper basket: you must rely on your instincts.

mechanical key on the golf course. In this way you can devote your total attention to how far you should hit the shot and to accuracy.

In practice, however, there are some points that you should concentrate on that will make you a better short-wedge player. You must be set up correctly. Keep your weight more on the left side, simply because it allows you to hit *down* more and, in addition, prevents you from swaying, which is fatal in a short-wedge situation. A slightly open stance will give better target perspective and will help restrict movement in your lower body.

Lower body movement *must* be kept to a minimum for optimum control. The legs and hips should not be totally restricted, just kept passive. Setting 60 percent of your weight on your left side, 40 percent on the right will accomplish this. Other fundamentals remain the same as for a full-wedge shot. The ball should be in the center of your stance, hands slightly ahead of it laterally.

The basic swing motion of a full-wedge shot must be retained on the half-wedge, but shortened. If you think of the shot as a half-swing you won't fear it. Most people faced with a short-wedge shot of thirty or forty yards get stiff and tight, thinking that some special effort is necessary to steer the ball to the target. They try to control the club too much in order to produce a straight shot. No chance. The only way to play a short shot well is to swing freely. And, as with the full wedge, to swing freely you must be relaxed and tempo-conscious. Relax and swing the clubhead smoothly through to the target.

Many players are so concerned with hitting the ball that they fail to swing through — which is their downfall. You've got to keep the clubhead *moving* through the impact area by making sure your hands

don't stop short of a hip-high finish. Remember, as long as your hands go forward, the clubhead will go toward the target. That's one secret to success around the green.

For a very short shot, a half-swing is all that is needed. Control the distance you hit the ball by the amount of force you put into this half-swing action.

THE LOW-FLYING PITCHING WEDGE

You'll see the touring professionals use this shot frequently. It can be used effectively from distances up to 80 yards in situations where you are playing into the wind, to a tight pin placement — in the back or close to the sides of the green under an overhanging tree limb; or it could be used when you need to make the ball carry to the top of a tiered green and stop quickly.

The secret of this shot is the massive amount of backspin you impart with a special action. You can expect the ball to take a couple of skips when it lands and stop abruptly.

In the setup, play the ball to the right of center, toward the right foot. Set your hands well ahead of the ball laterally to reduce the effect of loft on the clubface, which should be set square. Position your weight about 70 percent on your left side, 30 percent on your right, and keep it that way throughout the swing. This will cause a steep downswing arc, to give the ball a low flight trajectory.

A conscious effort is needed to make a more upright backswing than usual; take back the clubhead outside the target line. Follow this by leading your hands through the impact area well ahead of the clubhead. Delay the *release* — the pronation, or cross-over, of your hands at impact — as long as possible. Be sure to hit *down through* the shot. These changes will give you the low flight and the backspin essential to stop the ball quickly.

Be sure to keep your hands well ahead of the clubhead, through impact. Do not allow your wrists to release until well after impact.

THE PITCH-AND-RUN

You should use this shot when there is no pressing need to put the ball in the air, as when you face no obstructions such as bunkers or heavy grass between the ball and the hole. It's a great little percentage shot.

If you find yourself just off the green with the pin tucked in the rear portion, or you have to play either uphill or to a two-tiered placement, then you should run the ball. The closer you keep the ball to the ground the easier it is to gauge distance. That's important to remember. The less green you have to work with, the more you should pitch the ball. The more green that you have to work with, the more you roll the ball.

There are two clubs that can be used effectively for the pitch-and-run: the 5- and 7-irons. The farther you are from the pin, the more you will tend to use the less-lofted 5-iron, because you'll want to roll the ball. When the pin is close to you or where you need to negotiate fringe of anywhere from, say, six to ten feet, then the 7-iron should be used for more height and a little less roll.

Play the ball in the center of your stance and choke up on the grip. Place the grip end of the club just ahead of the ball. Your feet should be placed open, angled to the left of the flag to give you better ball/target perspective.

Now to the swing: Take the club back, keeping the face square. Very little wristbreak, other than a natural break, is required. It's more of a one-piece takeaway, where everything moves off the ball together.

On the downswing, make a conscious effort to keep your hands moving forward toward the target and the arms straight. Consciously point the club at the target on the follow-through. As long as the hands

To set up for a low-flying wedge shot that stops quickly, play the ball well to the right of center. Set your hands well ahead of the ball laterally and position your weight solidly on the left side.

keep going forward, the clubhead will too. *Quitting* — stopping the hands once the ball has been struck — is a common tendency. By focusing on leading the hands through to the target, there is no possible chance of a quit occurring.

Another helpful way to produce solid contact as well as consistency is to try to keep the clubhead low to the ground through impact to the finish. This will prevent any chance of lifting up and topping the shot.

Putting

There are basically two methods of putting: wrist putting and no-wrist putting. You must experiment to find which suits your game the best. Since there are both good wrist and good no-wrist putters, there is no ideal stroke. However, in careful study of a majority of the world's greatest putters, I have noticed that nearly all have very little wrist action. This is the method that I advocate and the one I use myself.

I feel that the fewer moving parts in the stroke, the less likelihood there is of error. There's too much movement in a wristy stroke. Wristy putters tend to be very streaky — one minute they hole putts from all over the place, the next they are three-putting. A no-wrist putter is generally more consistent.

Just as in the full swing, to putt well you first must have a good grip. The grip that I suggest is the *reverse-overlap*, in which the index finger of the left

I recommend a reverse-overlap grip, because it puts all the fingers of your right hand on the shaft. Your eyes should be directly over the ball.

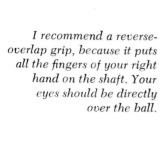

In the putting grip that I suggest, your palms are parallel to the putter face. This grip is readily achieved by aligning your thumbs straight down the center of the clubshaft. Position the ball in line with your left foot.

hand is placed over the uppermost two fingers of the right. This locks the hands together and puts all the fingers of the right hand on the grip of the club, which is important since the fingertips of the right hand harbor all the sensitivity and feel. The left thumb points directly down the shaft. Again, I am not suggesting that this reverse-overlap grip is the best putting grip for everyone. Far from it. If you prefer to hold the putter differently, go ahead. I would caution you, though, no matter what variation of finger and hand position you use, be sure and align your thumbs down the very center of your putter grip. This will give you the palm position essential for control. If your palms are parallel to the plane of the putter face when it is correctly aligned perpendicular to the line of the putt, all you have to worry about is making sure your hands work correctly. You can putt better by concentrating on only one thing (your hands) rather than two (your hands *and* the putter blade).

Also, in the putting address you should have your eyes directly over the ball so you can strike it solidly. Rather than bending a lot from the waist, you can accomplish this by standing closer to the ball. After assuming whatever posture is most comfortable for you, be sure that your eyes are over the ball and that the putter blade is aligned properly, square to the line of the putt, before you draw back the putter blade. The ball should be played either off your left heel or toe.

The only moving parts in the putting stroke are the shoulders, arms, and hands. Everything else, especially the head, remains perfectly still. A prime cause of an inconsistent stroke when putting is movement of the head — looking up too soon to see whether the ball is heading for the hole.

Make a conscious effort to keep the palms square to the line of the putt during both the backstroke and the follow-through. Again, remember: if your palms remain square to the line of the putt throughout, then the putter blade will, too.

A useful way to consistently produce solid contact — to make the putter face strike the ball squarely in the sweet spot — is to keep the blade low to the ground during backstroke and follow-through. This is something you can practice before playing. Try to make the putter head brush the surface of the grass, back and through.

Once you have perfected your own style of putting, there are really only two things to think of when you putt: the line and the speed. No other thoughts need concern you.

READING GREENS

You should start to read the breaks in the green long before you ever reach the green itself, because you can see undulations better from a distance; you can see whether the cup is set at an angle, or if there is even a slight change in the contour of the ground. From a distance, your eyes function like a carpenter's level and you get a broad perspective of the putt facing you.

Furthermore, as you approach the green you'll be able to check to see how the grain will affect your putt. Though most golfers ignore it, the grain often affects the putt just as much as the break. In some cases the grain may even offset the break. Be wary: check for grain.

Grain is best described as the way the grass lies. If the grass leans to the left, the ball will be influenced to roll in that direction. The opposite is true if the

A

B

C

grass leans to the right. When the grass leans toward you, you are putting against the grain, and your putt will be considerably slower than normal. You'll have to give a little extra to get the ball to the hole. You can tell from a distance when you face a putt against the grain: the grass will appear dull, patchy, dark in color. The opposite is true — the grass will be shinier and lighter — if you are putting downgrain. The ball will roll more when the grain is with you and you don't have to hit as hard.

HOW TO DEVELOP A CONSISTENT PUTTING STROKE

(A) You should start to read the break in your putt long before you get to the green. It is much easier to see the subtleties in the terrain from a distance.

(B) If the grass shines (as at left), then the grain is with you. If it's dark and patchy (right), the grain runs against you.

(C) Remember: when the grain goes against you (top drawing), hit the putt harder. Putting downgrain (bottom drawing), stroke the ball with less force than you'd use normally.

The drill shown on page 66 will help "groove" your putting stroke or, if you have been putting badly, will cure the yips. I have used this exercise with considerable success teaching amateurs at my club and when advising professional golfers who have had putting problems. Primarily, it teaches you how to make an *uninhibited* stroke. It also teaches you how critical it is (for most good putters) to keep *wrist action* out of the stroke.

Place your left hand as close to the bottom of the club's grip as you can without putting your fingers on the shaft. You'll find the large expanse of grip above your left hand will then rest against the fleshy part of your forearm. Now clamp your right hand over both your forearm and the handle. (See the illustration to be sure you are doing this correctly.)

Stroke a few putts, keeping the grip locked solidly against your arm. Notice that your wrists are completely uninvolved in the stroke and that the putter feels like an extension of your left arm. You want the feeling that you are making this left arm/putter

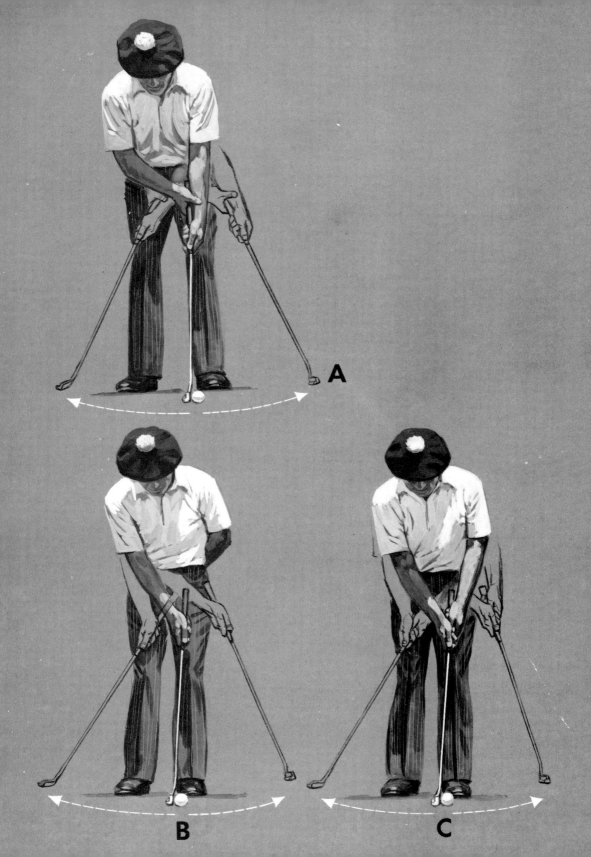

A

B

C

(A) Grasp the base of the club's grip with your left hand and clamp your right hand over the grip and your left forearm. Strike a few putts this way to get used to the feeling.

(B) Reverse the procedure. This time grasp with your right hand, but put your left hand behind you. Strike a few putts. Notice that the putter blade swings through unrestricted.

(C) Now use both hands. If there is any wristiness in the stroke, you'll notice it immediately and can correct it.

unit go through to the hole. You'll be amazed at the percentage of putts you hole from a short distance using this exercise method.

Next, to develop an unrestricted stroke, place your right hand on the handle in the same place you just had your left hand. This time, though, put your left arm behind your back. Using just your right hand, stroke a few putts. Notice that the putter blade goes through to the hole unrestricted each time; there is no left hand in the way to make it do otherwise. Use your right hand for a few minutes and you'll develop uncanny accuracy!

After practicing the left- and right-hand portions of the exercise, place both hands on the putter using your normal putting grip and stroke a few putts. You will be aware of any unwanted wristiness in the motion and can correct it; you'll also tend to follow through better, making the blade go through to the hole. Your stroke will be a lot smoother, a lot longer, and a lot less inhibited.

One last point, regarding a similar drill: Spend time putting with just the left hand (place the right behind you). This tip can be most helpful in eliminating any tendency to steer the putter blade toward the hole. Whether you practice with the right or left hand alone you'll no doubt be amazed at the putts you drop.

4

Bad Shots and How to Cure Them

Amateur's Note

No golfer plays the game without sometimes making bad shots. The exquisite, superdelicate timing, tempo, and control required for perfect shots every time can only be accomplished by a machine. No mortal can apply his or her limited physical abilities to the game — let alone confront the devilish effects of of golf's mental *strains* — and seriously expect errorless execution on every shot.

One of the most frustrating aspects of the game is to repeat a basic error — a hook, a slice, a shank, et cetera — and feel helpless and inadequate in searching for the necessary correction. We all flounder, experiment, overcompensate, grasp at straws . . . and often accept the inevitable. "OK," we righthanders say, "if I'm doomed to slice, I'll just aim each shot well to the left and let nature take its course."

Nature does *take its course* — resulting in the "banana-ball flight." But you needn't fight the laws of physics. (In fact, the more doggedly you compensate for error instead of correcting your technique, the more grievous and harder it will be to change your swing.) Our suggestion: refer in this chapter to the bad shot that most often plagues you and, next time out, try to apply the cure. Then, as others from the eleven categories of bad shots described here begin to threaten your game, you can develop confidence by knowing the truth, which will enable you to attempt to apply the right correction rather than meekly accept the bad shot.

Craig's advice is simple and to the point:

"Know the cause, then apply the cure.

"Don't be fooled into thinking that a misplayed

shot is a solitary happening. Your off-key swing, if you'll understand the whys and wherefores, has a message for you.

"Don't let bad shots terrorize you, and don't let bad breaks destroy your confidence or optimism. Instead of dwelling moodily on bad shots, you should analyze your swing for possible error. The next shot, then, can contain corrective measures rather than despair over the last poor shot.

"Obviously, you should absorb, analyze, and try to reason why the shot was mishit. But don't overreact or overcompensate. If you think positively, you'll be surprised at how your natural correction reactions — smooth, calm, unhurried — will result in that next shot being to your liking."

Slicing

A *slice* results when the clubhead crosses the target line from out to in, with the clubface in an open position at impact. This action causes a large amount of clockwise ball spin, resulting in a curve to the right.

The player who slices usually has two visible faults in his or her address position: (1) a "weak" grip — one with the hands turned too far to the left on the handle; and (2) a poorly aligned body, aimed well to the left of the intended target.

During the swing, a slicing tendency can be caused by moving over the top of the ball with the right shoulder; instead of the proper rotation under the

(A) A slice results when the clubhead moves across the target line from out to in, with the clubface in an open position at impact.

(B) Making a grip change can have a drastic effect on the path the clubhead follows. With a proper grip the clubhead will approach the ball along the correct path and meet the ball squarely.

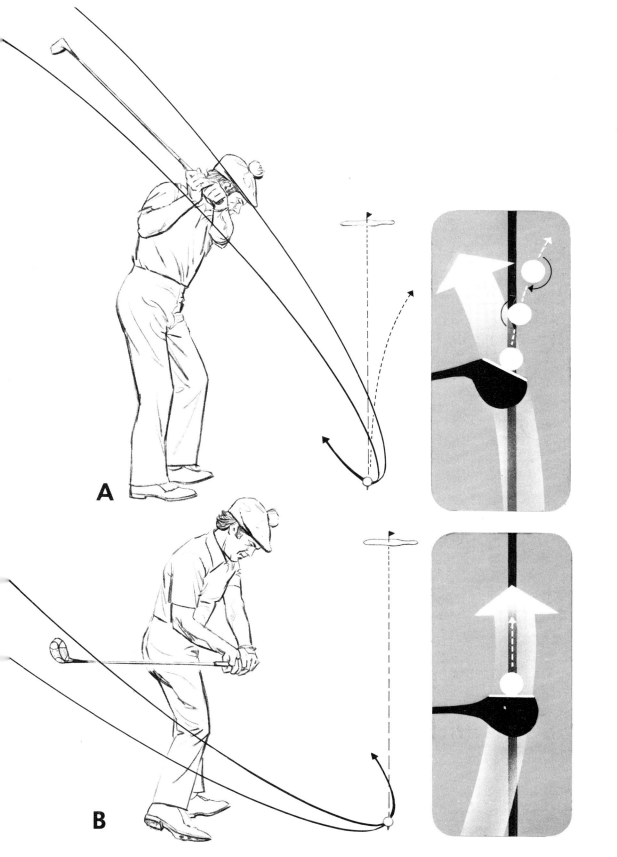

A

B

chin, the right shoulder turns into the follow-through on a more horizontal plane. Another common cause of slicing is failing to release — to pronate the hands through the impact area. If the right hand doesn't turn over the left, the clubface will remain in an open position. It's also possible that the clubface could be open at address, causing a slice upon impact.

I have found that a slicing tendency usually stems from a "weak" grip, which causes the clubface to open more than it should during the swing. Since the clubface will be an open position at impact if the hands are turned too far left on the club's grip, the player must eventually compensate by aiming to the left and using his or her right side to prevent a massive banana ball. Of course, a right-sided swing with open alignment only compounds the fault by forcing the clubhead even farther outside the line and turning the clubface into an even more open position.

If you slice, remember that the ball reacts to the face of the club, to its position at the point of impact. Logically, to cure a slice you first must look to the part of your body that directly controls the clubface: your hands.

I have eliminated slicing with tremendous success by making players who slice change from their "weak" grip to a "strong" one and then gradually back to an orthodox position. Slicers trying a strong grip immediately see the influence hand position has on the pattern of their shots; most of the time they abruptly cease slicing and start to hook consistently. Then, as they get used to seeing the ball travel to the left, I gradually move their hands back into a more orthodox position (see pages 13–19 for a full description of the standard grip) and shots begin to straighten out.

If you're trying to correct a slice, I encourage you to try a grip change first. Once you have established the correct grip, there will no longer be any need for alignment compensations: your stance and the clubface can be aimed square to your target. Having used an open position for so long, a change to square alignment will at first feel strange. But as you consistently hit straight shots you'll gain more confidence.

If you have a good grip and find you still slice, then the fault obviously must be in your swing. Once you have set yourself up at address properly, the fastest way to eliminate a slice is to consciously make your right hand turn over your left (release) through the hitting area. If you force your hands to pronate, the clubface will close passing through the impact area, resulting in counterclockwise spin and a shot that if anything will hook rather than slice. Making a conscious effort to release, you may even find you pull the first few shots you hit. Just allow this to happen. Because of the increased understanding you'll have of the function that your hands perform in the swing, it won't be long before your swing begins to follow the correct path.

Hooking

A *hook* is caused by the clubhead crossing the target line from in to out, with the clubface in a closed position at impact. This causes counterclockwise spin on the ball and results in a sharp curve to the left. The ball reacts both to the direction in which

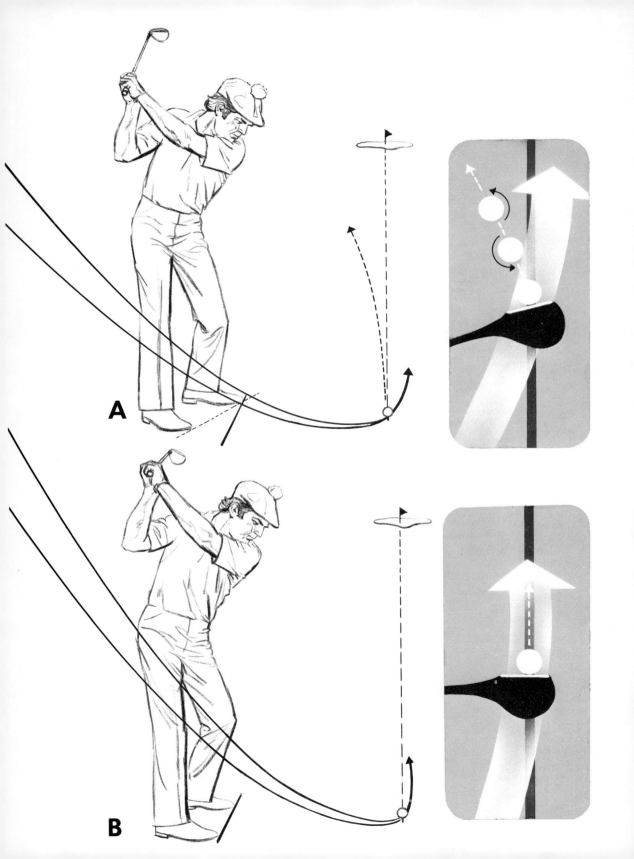

A

B

the clubhead is traveling and to the angled position of the clubface at impact.

Most players react to a hooking tendency by aiming farther to the right of the target. As the hook becomes more pronounced, such players aim farther to the right. This forces them to take the club back even farther to the inside and to use their right side to close the clubface more, just to get the ball back in play. Of course, the more the clubhead approaches the ball from the inside with the face in a closed position, the greater the counterclockwise spin and the more the ball will hook. Eventually, the problem becomes so serious the golfer must start fighting to prevent a *duck hook* — a short, diving hook.

To eliminate a hook, delve to the root of the fault: the grip. Then concentrate on other sound fundamentals that will help you return the clubface to the ball in a square position. But you must first realize that the hooking habit took a long time to become ingrained and will take a long time to correct.

The most common cause of hooking is too "strong" a grip — one where the hands are turned too far to the right on the handle of the club. The left hand, instead of showing two knuckles beyond the left wrist, shows three or four, and the inverted V's formed by the fingers and thumbs point to the right of the player's right shoulder. Unfortunately, the player's swing, from address through finish, will build around this one fault in trying to compensate for it.

Changing from a "strong" grip to an orthodox position will feel uncomfortable and "weak" at first. You will undoubtedly have to suffer through a few bad shots until your muscle memory absorbs the new feeling. However, once this is accomplished you will

(A) A hook is caused by the clubhead moving in an exaggerated inside-to-outside arc across the target line, resulting in a closed clubface at impact. The follow-through arc then fails to continue on line to the target.

(B) A grip correction and a conscious effort to swing the clubhead along the target line will help to eliminate the hook.

agree that the sacrifice was worth it. (Refer to pages 13–19 for a thorough description of the proper grip.)

At address, be sure that the clubhead sits flat on the ground with the clubface square to the target. If the toe of the clubhead is in the air, the heel will catch the ground first, forcing the clubface to twist closed on impact. Be sure that your shoulders are aligned parallel to the target line, since they influence the path the clubhead follows. If they were closed, angled to the right of the target, you would be forced to use your right side to compensate and would hook the ball. Your toes should also be parallel to the target line; in all respects, address the ball squarely.

In the takeaway, allow the clubhead to follow the natural turn of your shoulders. And in the downswing, swing the clubhead through toward, not away from, the target. If the clubhead travels down the target line for as long as possible, the ball will not deviate off line much, even if the face of the club is slightly open or closed.

Since the hook is a right-side dominated fault, you must insure that the left side remains the controlling factor throughout the downswing. This is readily accomplished by clearing your left side out of the way first to trigger the downswing. Then the clubhead and your hands will be following your lower body through the impact area and will not get ahead of it. "Beat the club, don't let it beat you."

KEYS TO CORRECT HOOKING

1. Check your grip. Is it too "strong"? Correct it.
2. Be sure your alignment is square.
3. Swing to target.
4. Develop more left-side control on the downswing.

Topping

When the clubhead travels through the impact area on the upswing and strikes the top half of the ball, the shot will be *topped*. Instead of contacting the ball at the low point of the downswing, the clubhead is moving up as it strikes the ball. The result: the ball is struck with either the leading edge or the soleplate of the clubhead and it never fully compresses on the clubface.

If this is your problem, your mistake could be:

● Looking at the target before hitting the ball.

● Jerking the club back from the ball in the backswing.

● Tensing up in the address position and thus overcontrolling the club during the swing.

● Moving your hub (head, neck, and shoulders) upward from its original address position.

● Staying back on your right side, so that you have too much weight on your right foot at impact (see pages 35–36).

● Positioning the ball too far left in the address.

If you are consistently topping the ball but can't isolate your particular fault, I can almost guarantee that your problem lies in the address. Tension in the forearms, wrists, and hands will cause overcontrol to set in. The tension will prevent the clubhead from swinging freely in its natural arc, and the swing will in effect become a totally right-handed motion. Be sure not to grip the club too tightly, since this is the principal cause of tension, and keep your knees flexed, not stiff.

Focus on good balance in the address position and on smoothness throughout the entire swing. There is a routine that I suggest to my students to help ac-

> **KEYS TO CORRECT TOPPING**
>
> 1. Don't be too tense; relax.
> 2. Avoid too much weight on your left side at the top of the backswing.
> 3. Avoid too much weight on your right side at impact.
> 4. Guard against bad posture; flex your knees.
> 5. Don't overreach.
> 6. Insure extension; keep your left arm straight.
> 7. Don't swing too quickly; be smooth.

complish natural movement: from the time you select the club from the bag until the finish of your swing, make your movements smooth and deliberate. Don't hurry. In aligning your feet and looking from the target or target-line marker spot back to the ball, move with rhythm and smoothness.

During the swing itself, be sure to keep your head still. This is the most basic and undoubtedly the best way to cure a topping problem. If you continually raise your head or move it to the right, sooner or later you will top some shots. Keep your head still and allow your shoulders to turn.

Another precaution you can take in the swing is to make a conscious effort to pull the club down with the left hand leading. If you keep your left hand in

Don't be tense in your address. Having your knees rigid or allowing tension in your upper body can lead to a fast, jerky swing.

Keep your knees flexed and your arms and hands tension-free.

mind, you'll prevent your right hand and right side from dominating. Check your ball position, keep a steady head position and a smooth, unhurried swing — and you'll quickly kiss your topping problem good-bye.

Shanking

A *shank* is undoubtedly the most feared shot in golf. Once you have hit one you are always wary that you'll hit another. Unfortunately, the more you fear a shank, the more likely it is to happen, which is one reason why many players have a stretch of several shanked shots.

KEYS TO CORRECT SHANKING

1. Eliminate tension; grip the club lightly.
2. Balance yourself properly; be sure your weight is on the balls of your feet.
3. Swing the club; don't steer it.
4. Don't stand too close to ball at address.
5. Release your hands freely at ball impact; don't block the shot.
6. Pull your hands through toward your belt buckle.

You shank when the ball is struck by the hozel, the round part where the shaft is joined with the clubhead. The result is a shot that shoots off at a sharp angle to the right.

A shank will occur more often around the green than on longer shots, because on short shots you may tend to try *too* hard to get the ball close to the hole. Instead of swinging freely, you become tense and try to *steer* the clubhead toward the hole. This tension and inhibited swing result in a failure to release your hands — they remain well ahead of the clubhead, which arrives at the point of impact with the face wide open.

I consider tension and steering the primary causes of shanking. Both can force the clubhead out of its natural arc. In other words, while the clubface will start in the ideal position, with the ball in the center

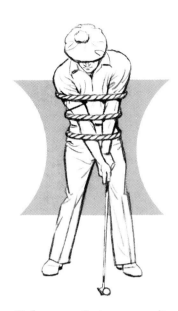

Make sure that you aren't bound with tension in your address.

The most common cause of shanking is looping the clubhead outside the target line. You can see here, both from an overhead and rear view, what happens to the clubhead in the backswing and downswing. The insets show why the ball leaves the clubhead at a sharp angle to the right.

of the face at address, at impact the clubhead will have returned with the face outside the ball. This is because the club was taken back on a reasonably sound path but then, either because of tension or an attempt to steer the ball, it was forced to make a big loop outside of its natural arc.

Though the most common cause of shanking is looping to the outside, you can also shank if the clubhead moves into the hitting area from a sharp inside path. (This isn't quite as common, although it also stems from tension or steering.) Other causes include standing too close to the ball at address, gripping the club too tightly, turning the clubface wide open in the backswing so that you are unable to close it in the downswing, or shifting too much weight to your toes while swinging through the impact area.

Before I discuss the many possible cures, I should point out that some will work for one player and not for another. I encourage you to experiment until you find the one that works consistently for you.

To correct a shank, the first step is to quiet your mind. Forecast a positive result. Picture clearly a smooth tempo, a solid strike, and the ball landing by the hole. Positive thought breeds positive action. This done, focus on your address position.

Relax and don't crowd the ball: stand farther away than normal. If you have been hitting the ball on the hozel, the most logical way to contact the ball squarely on the clubface is to stand back. In extreme shanking cases, I even go so far as to instruct a student to stand farther away from the ball and attempt to hit it off the toe of the clubhead. I realize that this is going from one extreme to the other, but it's the fastest way to stop shanking, and it makes the player conscious of what he or she has to do to make solid contact: make the downswing path almost duplicate the backswing path.

Position the ball in the center of the clubface and don't grip too tightly. Your weight should rest on your heels and remain there throughout the swing. If your weight starts on your toes, or shifts forward when the swing is in motion, then the path of your downswing will also move forward (see chapter two), bringing the hozel of the club into play.

You can prevent the clubface from *spreading*, becoming too open in the takeaway, by envisioning an imaginary straight line between the target and the ball. Just make the clubhead stay on the line, with the clubface at right angles to it. This will insure a square position.

Overall, the swing should be smooth. Don't be afraid to release your hands. Remember, once you have hit the ball you can't do a thing about it. Don't try to steer, or overcontrol, the clubhead; let it swing naturally.

I'm not a great believer in gimmicks, but in the case of a serious and frustrating fault like shanking, I do use one or two tricks to eliminate the problem. For example, I'll often place a block of wood or a second golf ball approximately one inch from the ball to be hit, outside the target line, and have pupils try a shot. Players who have been shanking will usually hit the wood or the marker ball first, since their downswing arcs approach sharply either from the outside or from the inside. The shock of impact quickly makes them realize their fault. Then, I ask that they imagine that they are pulling their hands in toward their belt buckle through impact. When they are able to miss the wooden block or the marker ball and strike the shot solidly, I remove the ob-

Relaxing grip pressure and standing farther away from the ball will help alleviate the danger of shanking.

Place a block of wood about an inch from the ball, outside the target line, and try hitting. When the clubhead misses the wood, there's no way you can shank a shot. A second golf ball, placed one inch from the ball to be hit, can substitute for the wood.

stacle and make them repeat the shot. Most of the time, any tendency to shank disappears.

Skulling, Thinning, or Hitting Daisy-Cutters

If I were to rank the most frequently hit bad shots, *skulling, thinning, or hitting daisy-cutters* would follow right after shanking. These three shots — low, screaming, ground-huggers — are joined under one heading because all have the same cause.

There you are, sitting pretty either just in front of the green or in good shape to play your second shot in, and what happens? Instead of that nice, floating trajectory that you had hoped for, followed by the ball landing softly on the green, you get a low screamer that barely gets off the ground.

Why does the ball assume such a low trajectory? What happened that caused it to fly over the green? Your clubhead contacted the ball above the center and as it was moving up. (A "skulled" shot goes much farther and lower than planned; a "topped" shot, which has a similar cause, is a dribbler that gets no distance.)

In most cases this fault is caused by lifting the head (hub) up as the clubhead swings through the impact area. When your hub lifts, the low point of your swing moves up also (see chapter two). Thus, it is the leading edge of the clubhead rather than the clubface that makes contact with the ball. The club-face can only make proper contact if the leading edge of the club strikes the bottom half of the ball

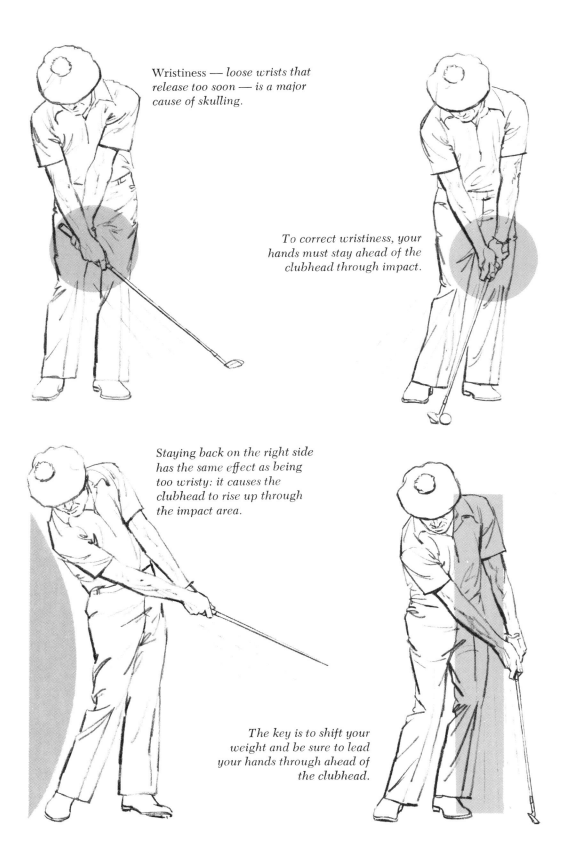

Wristiness — *loose wrists that release too soon* — *is a major cause of skulling.*

To correct wristiness, your hands must stay ahead of the clubhead through impact.

Staying back on the right side has the same effect as being too wristy: it causes the clubhead to rise up through the impact area.

The key is to shift your weight and be sure to lead your hands through ahead of the clubhead.

at the point of impact. The ball then spins up the face and gains height.

The only way to insure solid contact is to keep your head/hub still throughout the swing, especially during impact. To help yourself "stay down," so to speak, keep your eyes focused on the ball's ID number or on the manufacturer's name. You can work on this a lot in practice. Set the ball so its imprint faces away from the target and is just within sight during address; then keep your eyes focused on the writing until the ball is airborne.

Another cause of these low-flying shots is swinging too fast, especially under pressure. Be conscious of your tempo and try for smoothness, not speed. With a steady head and a smooth swing, you'll be able to feel that the clubhead is still descending until the ball is airborne. If you are too "wristy" or fail to shift your weight, you're inviting a skulled shot.

One of the best ways to ingrain the feeling of solid contact when hitting irons is to practice *punch shots*. On the practice tee, practice "hitting down" and abbreviating your follow-through to about waist height. This will train you to hit down, not up.

Finally, when you are on the course playing a match, be sure to pick a club that will give you the distance you require. Don't *ever* force a club. To force a club you must speed up your swing — and I've already outlined the problems that will create. Rather than force a club, it is better to select a lower-numbered one and slow down the overall speed of your swing.

> KEYS TO CORRECT
> SKULLING, THINNING,
> OR HITTING
> DAISY-CUTTERS
>
> 1. Don't be loose and overly wristy; keep your hands ahead of the clubhead through impact.
> 2. Don't straighten up before impact; keep your hub steady.
> 3. Remember tempo; make your overall swing smooth.
> 4. Hit down and finish low.
> 5. Be sure to shift your weight to the left side.

Pulling

A *pulled* shot — one that travels to the left without curving — results when the clubhead travels along a line that points to the left of the intended target, with the clubface aimed squarely in that same direction. This fault can happen with any club and on all shots, even short pitches, chips, and putts, and does not necessarily result from a bad swing. In fact, if the swing on a pulled shot is reasonably good and the ball is struck solidly, the only missing ingredient is the right direction.

Pulled shots can be caused by:

● Standing too far away from the ball.

● Playing the ball too far forward, with the shoulders misaligned toward the left of the target.

● Failing to complete the shoulder turn on the backswing.

● Allowing the clubhead to approach the ball from too far outside the target line.

● Omitting leg action in the swing.

● Rushing the overall tempo of the swing.

In the address, check to see that you aren't overreaching. Your arms should be comfortably extended, but not rigid and too straight. Keep the upper half of your arms resting lightly against your sides.

Be sure also that the ball isn't too far forward, to the left of your left heel. This causes the shoulders to misalign to the left. Your shoulders have the greatest influence on the path of the clubhead through the impact area.

Throughout the backswing be especially conscious of completing your shoulder-turn. Although incorrect, it is very easy, especially in a crucial situation, to shorten your backswing. Your left shoulder should

---

KEYS TO CORRECT PULLING

1. Don't overreach; stand closer to the ball.
2. Align yourself properly; be sure your shoulders are parallel to the target line.
3. Check ball position: Is it too far forward?
4. Check your shoulders at impact: Are they in a square position?

A primary cause of pulling is standing too far away from the ball.

Be sure that you aren't overreaching. Your arms should be comfortably extended.

Failing to turn the shoulders on the backswing is another common cause of pulling.

At the top of your backswing, your left shoulder should be under your chin and your back should be facing the target.

be under your chin and your back should face the target at the top of the backswing. A good backswing shoulder-turn sets up the proper stroke plane and the correct downswing path. The clubhead will be inclined to follow more of an inside than an outside arc into the ball.

In the downswing, the lower body must lead the hands. If the knees are used properly, moving toward the target laterally, you will block out any chance of an early release of the hands that would force the clubhead out of the correct path and cause the clubface to close. For the same reason, be especially conscious of your overall tempo; if it is too fast, the clubhead will be thrown out of line by your wrists and will arrive at the ball ahead of your lower body, in a closed position.

One final note: During practice, check your shoulder position at impact by swinging the club to the top of your backswing, then down, and freeze at the point of impact. Your shoulders should be perfectly square, parallel to the target line. If not, keep practicing until you arrive at the ball in a square-shoulders position. When you accomplish this, try hitting the ball. You'll find that you return instinctively to the square-shoulders position, and the pulling tendency will diminish.

Pushing

A *pushed shot* — one that travels to the right without curving — results from the clubhead in the follow-through swinging out to the right of the target, with the clubface aimed squarely in that direction. Like a pulled shot, the swing is not necessarily bad — the ball can be struck solidly and travel far — it just lacks proper direction.

If the swing is indeed correct, an obvious cause of pushing could be misalignment — for example, when the shoulders are aligned aiming directly *at* the target, instead of *parallel* to the ball's imaginary target line. Also, positioning the ball too far back in the stance can result in a push.

You can easily check to see if your shoulder alignment is at fault. Assume your address position, then freeze. Take the club and run the shaft across your shoulder blades. If you find the club points either directly toward or to the right of the target, simply pull your left shoulder back slightly until your shoulders are parallel to the intended flight path (target line) of the ball.

One other common cause of a push is the lower body getting too far ahead of the hands in the downswing. This is largely the result of bad tempo — failure to synchronize the movement of the upper and lower body — and can be cured by a slower, more controlled takeaway.

My final point, and undoubtedly the golden key to eliminating the push, is to concentrate on making the clubhead move out along the target line after the ball has been struck. Remember: swing the clubhead along the target line and through to the target.

> KEYS TO CORRECT
> PUSHING
> 1. Check alignment; your shoulders should be parallel to the ball's target line, not aimed *at* target.
> 2. Check ball position: Is it too far back?
> 3. Don't rush or jerk the downswing hip-turn.
> 4. Swing to target.

Skying, or Popping Up

A shot that is *skied*, or *popped up*, generally lands short: it virtually goes nowhere except up. This is a frustrating dilemma common to wood shots, from the tee or fairway. In either case, the fault is caused by an extreme downward, chopping-type blow that contacts the ball not with the clubface, but with the polished surface of the top of the clubhead. The player who consistently skies the ball can easily be recognized by the clubheads of his woods, which are freckled with white marks.

Let's take a look at how those white marks get there. The following are possible causes:

● Gripping the club too tightly.

● Shifting too much weight to your left side at the top of your backswing.

● Using your right hand excessively during the swing.

● Moving your head and dipping the hub downward.

● Bringing the club down into the impact area too steeply, from outside the target line.

When using a driver from the tee, a player's first reaction to a skied shot is to tee the ball lower. While this serves as a psychological aid, it usually does not cure the fault. A pop-up is usually not caused by a high tee, but rather by a steep downswing arc — the clubhead descends toward the ball at a sharp angle. A player who consistently skies his tee shots will almost certainly sky his fairway wood shots. The cure, then, must be to eliminate the faults which lead to this steep downswing arc. A review of the basics is necessary.

First: position the ball off your left heel on all

Two causes of skying are having the ball too far back toward your right foot in the address and shifting your weight too quickly to your left side during the downswing. Each results in the clubhead approaching the ball at too steep an angle.

Play the ball off your left heel, and make a conscious effort to sweep the clubhead through the impact area on a level plane.

KEYS TO CORRECT
SKYING, OR POPPING UP

1. Eliminate tension in your address; relax!
2. Keep your weight equally balanced at the start.
3. Avoid an abrupt pickup; keep the club low in your takeaway.
4. Keep your head still; watch out for a dipping hub.
5. Sweep the ball; don't chop at it.
6. Play the ball more off your left heel at address.
7. Use less right-hand force during the swing.

wood shots; extend your left arm to provide maximum width of arc, which in turn will result in the essential sweeping action. Second: hold the club as if there were eggs in both your hands — firmly but not tightly — and position your hands slightly ahead of the ball laterally at address. (Players who grip too tightly or position their hands behind the ball at address will be inclined to pick up the club in a jerky fashion with the right hand dominating the backswing.) Distribute your weight equally between both feet.

Once again, I cannot stress enough the importance of a steady head during the swing. Don't allow your head to shift, wobble, or turn. Imagine that you are balancing a tray of cups on your head throughout the backswing and downswing. But most important of all, be sure that at the top of your backswing the bulk of your weight is on your right side. If your weight is on the left, then you will be forced to use your right hand in the downswing and the result will be another skied shot.

Overall, try to imagine that you are about to *sweep* the ball off the tee or the ground. I observe many of my pupils on the first tee practicing swinging with their drivers and taking huge divots. This is not only bad for the tee area — it ingrains a fault into their swings.

The key is to avoid hitting down with the woods and to sweep instead. To convey the importance of this to my students, especially those who are skying the ball, I tee up a ball *extra* high for them. Then I ask that they try hitting the ball several times while attempting to leave the tee in the ground. This quickly alleviates the tendency to hit down and, to their amazement, the skying problem disappears.

If skying is your problem, ask yourself: What's the

opposite of chopping? The answer is, of course, sweeping — it will stop popping up.

Smothering

A *smothered* shot is best described as a shot that barely leaves the ground and veers to the left. This often occurs when a player is under pressure to win a match, is on a tight hole, or needs a par on the last hole to score the best round of his life.

The cause of smothering is an overdominant right side, which forces the clubhead to close and to cross the target line from outside to inside at impact. The right side dominates in pressure situations because the player is so tense he tends to steer the ball instead of allowing the club to swing freely, and he shifts too much weight to the left side too early in the swing. As a result, the player leans toward the target and is unable to clear his left side effectively without over-using his right side.

To cure this problem — as with any major fault in the swing — you must first check to see that your setup is correct. Your first consideration must be the grip. Be sure that you aren't using too "strong" a hold on the club. The V's should be pointing to your right shoulder, not to the right of it.

Next, be sure that the clubface is aimed square to the target, not closed. The soleplate of the club should be flat on the ground. If the toe of the club is in the air — if there is a gap between the toe and the ground — the heel will catch the turf first and cause the clubface to close. Position the ball off your

Smothering is caused by an overdominant right side that forces the clubhead to close and to cross the target line moving toward the inside on the follow-through.

A full shoulder-turn will prevent your right shoulder from going out over the top of the ball. Be sure to swing the clubhead toward the target on the follow-through.

KEYS TO CORRECT
SMOOTHERING

**KEYS TO CORRECT
SMOTHERING**

1. Check grip: Is your right-hand too tight? Grip lightly.
2. Keep the clubface square, not hooded.
3. Make a good shoulder-turn.
4. Remember target awareness; swing the clubhead toward the target on follow-through.

left heel when hitting woods and long irons, and in the middle of your stance when hitting other clubs. Having the ball too far back can cause a smothered shot, because the clubhead approaches the impact area at a steep angle of descent. (The smothered shot results from the clubhead coming *down on* the ball; a "skied" shot results from the club coming *down under* the ball.) Lifting the club by breaking the wrists too quickly in the takeaway will have the same effect as positioning the ball too far back.

A conscious effort to make a good shoulder-turn will insure that the clubhead *sweeps* back away from the ball and is not "picked up." Besides the shoulder-turn, a good extension of the arms throughout the backswing will maintain a wide, sweeping arc.

To eliminate a smothering tendency, I make my students very target conscious, from the minute they address the ball. If your mind is not aware of where the target is, it will fail to *tell* your body how to guide the swing. Make yourself aware of where the target is, then attempt to swing the clubhead toward the target in the follow-through. Remember: the basic cause of a smothered shot is swinging the clubhead leftward rather than directly at the target.

**KEYS TO CORRECT
SCLAFFING**

1. Shift your weight from right foot to left before impact.
2. Avoid too much right hand; be smooth.

Sclaffing

The term *sclaffing*, which originated in Great Britain, means hitting too far behind the ball — although not in the same sense as on the *fat* shot. When you hit a fat shot, the clubface hits ground behind the ball (laterally) but doesn't contact the ball at all: the loosened turf lifts the ball into the air. A sclaff is almost a good shot because the face of the club does make contact; unfortunately, impact occurs *after* the clubhead has struck the ground. When this happens clubhead speed is reduced, resulting in loss of distance.

Sclaffing stems simply from failing to shift your weight during the downswing. Instead of moving your weight from right to left, you leave it on your right side. This causes your upper body to dominate, your hands to release early — and a sclaff.

Fortunately, the cure is as simple as the cause: just consciously move your knees laterally to start the downswing. This will make your lower body the leader throughout the downswing and will eliminate any chance of your upper body dominating. Also, be sure to swing smoothly and keep your right hand relaxed.

When my students have a sclaffing problem, I make them hit shots and "walk after" the ball — literally step forward with the right foot on the follow-through. The only way you can walk after a shot is to shift your weight correctly; the sclaffing problem is gone with the first step.

Failing to shift your weight to your left side and staying back on your right side will cause the clubhead to strike the ground first, resulting in a sclaffed shot.

Hitting the Fat Chip or Pitch

There is nothing more frustrating to a golfer than hitting a *fat* pitch or chip shot — one that catches too much turf before the ball, preventing clubface contact.

Use your knees to shift your weight laterally to the left, to be sure you hit the ball first.

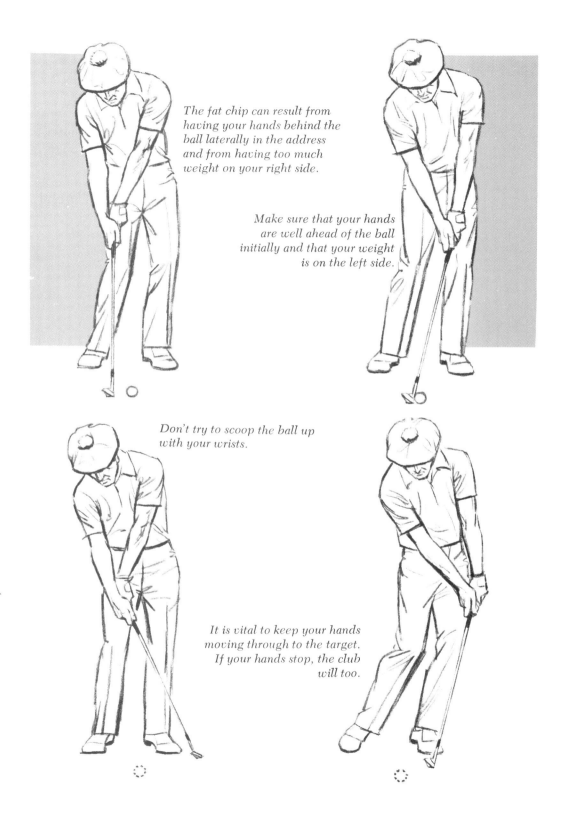

The fat chip can result from having your hands behind the ball laterally in the address and from having too much weight on your right side.

Make sure that your hands are well ahead of the ball initially and that your weight is on the left side.

Don't try to scoop the ball up with your wrists.

It is vital to keep your hands moving through to the target. If your hands stop, the club will too.

Fat shots can have several causes. Fear of playing a short shot off hard ground, for example, creates tension, which can cause overcontrol to set in — the clubhead is not allowed to swing freely. Other causes are:

- Taking a quick, jerky backswing.
- Scooping at the ball with your wrists.
- Using your arms only, without any lower body action.
- Having too much weight on your right foot at impact.
- Lifting your head up.
- Forgetting to stay conscious of where the target is located.

The address position is the key to overcoming fat shots. If you feel you are set up correctly, and you have the target and the type of shot you want to play clearly in mind, you will give no thought to mishitting the ball. Your stance should be slightly open, to give you a better ball-target perspective than the normal square stance provides. Play the ball in the center of your stance and set your weight to favor your left side. Place your hands well ahead of the ball laterally for a smooth takeaway.

Be sure not to grip the club too tightly or tension will spread into your arms; the buildup of tension destroys your natural tempo. A relaxed hold on the club will serve to calm you down and keep the overall motion smooth.

Most of the backswing movement should be controlled by your shoulders, arms, and hands, in that order. Keep your lower body relatively still.

KEYS TO CORRECT THE FAT CHIP OR PITCH

1. Correct your address; balance your weight on your left side.
2. Position your hands ahead of the ball at address.
3. Keep your arms, hands, and club moving through to target.

5

Basic Trouble Shots— Bunkers, Wind, Water, Rough— and How to Master Them

Amateur's Note

As a particularly pleasant part of the research for this book, I had the opportunity to play some of Scotland's finest courses — among them, Saint Andrews, Carnoustie, Gleneagles, Troon, and Turnbery — as a "partner/pupil" of Craig Shankland, our teaching pro. It was not just the advantage of playing eleven rounds in eight days — with dozens of hours of concentrated, on-the-course instruction from this outstanding teacher — that was so instructive; I also came to realize that the Scottish attitude toward the game is so pure and uplifting that we Sassanachs might well reflect upon and borrow from it in our own approach to golf.

I mention this as we come to the chapter "Trouble Shots and How to Master Them" (one of the most valuable chapters in the book, in my opinion), because the healthy Scottish approach to trouble shots especially deserves our admiration and imitation. The rough-and-tumble courses in Scotland bear little resemblance to our manicured greens and pampered fairways. Scottish golfers eagerly accept troublesome aspects such as wind, rain, wild rough, and cavernous bunkers, as basic elements of the game. They revel in the "trouble" rough weather and tough terrain offer and rejoice in the opportunity to execute new and unexpected shots.

For the golfers of Scotland there are no winter rules or improved lies. I sometimes think that too many of us in the United States are spoiled to the point that we take it as a personal affront, a dastardly trick of fate, when we don't end up with a perfect lie, or when we get a less-than-kindly kick, or when we hit a tree and, instead of bouncing into the fairway, veer into the deep rough. Who would really like a golf course where you always drive downwind and downhill, where there are no trees, bunkers, or rough to impede your progress, and where all greens are funnel-shaped, so that any shot to the vicinity of the flag rolls unerringly into the cup?

As for trouble shots, Craig prefers to call them challenge *or* recovery shots. *I agree, and hope you do, too. When your prospects look bleakest you should rise to the challenge, knowing that you* can *recover; your mind should tell you that all is not lost — that your swing can propel the ball to the target because you know the essence, theory, and technique of the shot. As soon as we accept the truism that in* any *round of golf we will inevitably find trouble and face challenging shots, we realize that these seemingly negative aspects of the game are really what give us the greatest positive feelings of accomplishment. When we conquer the trouble, meet the challenge, solve the problem and recover — that's when we deservedly experience the thrill of achievement.*

In tough situations you combine your mental preparation for a golfing round with your physical approach to individual on-the-course shots. If you know that trouble is inevitable, it's not such a brutal shock when it arrives. Remember: as surely as you will mishit a number of easy shots, you'll also invariably find your share of trouble shots on and off the fairway. You will, at times, land in the rough, confront precarious fairway lies, settle behind a tree, lodge in a hazard, bury in a bunker.

So this chapter on basic trouble shots and the chapter that follows on related problems are, we hope, "worth the price of admission." Use these chapters before you play to review and bone up on the situations that cause you the greatest headaches.

And also use the pointers here after *your round, to determine what you might have done to solve a recurrent problem. Next time out you will do better.*

Here are further thoughts for you from Craig:

"*Mere hope or an accidental swing can never be your salvation when you are faced with a difficult trouble shot or a formidable recovery situation. Some people take the easy way out: they put the ball in their pocket — pick up and, really, give up. Nothing could be more alien to the game's philosophy than a belief that all hope on a particular hole or on a particular shot is lost.*

"*Play it. Try it. Make the attempt. And, at worst, play the shot to a safe position and hope that your* next *shot will put you in position for a one-putt. This involves* planning ahead. *Visualize the next shot, and the one after that. Always have a target to shoot at, even when playing safe. Know what you want to do and where you want to go even before you hit that safe shot.*

"*And remember that there is no drastic mechanical swing change for even the most challenging trouble or recovery shots. Tempo, visualization, an unhurried attitude and swing — those are what add up to success.*"

Bunkers

The Basic Bunker Shot

The swing you use with a sand iron in the bunker is the same swing you would use with any other club. The length of the swing should not change (you use a full backswing) even though the distance the ball travels and the force that is used might. There are no drastic swing-plane changes in mid-swing. Fundamental changes in the address will, however, produce a cutting action — a natural swing in which the club-face remains slightly open and cuts through the sand on an out-to-in path. A complete knowledge of the necessary fundamentals will assist you in keeping your bunker swing rhythmic, smooth, and simple.

Set your feet in an open stance, shoulder-width apart. (An open stance is achieved by pulling your left foot back from the target line, so that a line drawn across your toes would intersect the target line at approximately a 45-degree angle.) Form a firm foundation for your swing by digging your feet in, wiggling them from side to side, until the sand feels solid beneath your heels. Just as a building would crumble if its foundations were not laid correctly, so will your swing if it doesn't have a solid base. As a result of digging in you will be lower in relation to the ball, so compensate by *choking up*

(A) On basic sand shots, always be sure to aim two inches behind the ball. Imagine that you are tossing the ball to a specific target on the green.

(B) Use an open stance for all standard bunker shots.

(C) On a long shot, try to take just a saucerful of sand beneath the ball.

(D) For a little less distance, take enough sand to fill a soup bowl.

(E) For a very short shot, take enough sand to fill a mixing bowl.

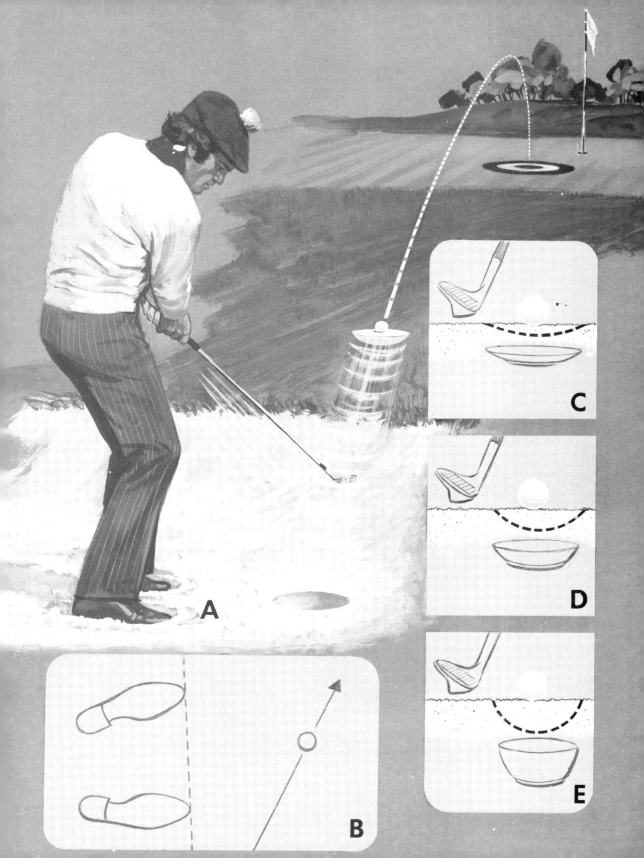

A

B

C

D

E

A

B

C

on the handle of the club: grip farther down the shaft. Position yourself so that the ball is in the center of your stance. Open the clubface and set your hands slightly ahead of the ball laterally. Having your hands forward will encourage a smoother, more controlled takeaway.

I have already mentioned that the length of swing should not change, regardless of the distance the ball must travel. What then enables you to control distance correctly? The answer: force within the swing and the amount of sand you make the clubface take under (not behind) the ball. Don't make the common mistake of changing the amount of sand taken *behind* the ball. Aim the clubhead at a spot two inches behind the ball, and vary the height and length of shots by the controlling amount of sand you take *under* the ball. If you need a long shot, hit shallow — imagine you are taking enough sand beneath the ball to fill a saucer. For a little less distance, hit deeper — take enough sand to fill a soup bowl. For a very short shot, hit deeper still — take enough sand to fill a mixing bowl. But in each case use the same length swing. A simple key: think *shallow for longer* shots and think *deep for shorter* distances. A conscious effort to make a full backswing is essential. The best bunker players in the world all make a full shoulder-turn, so that the club is a little short of the horizontal position at the top of the backswing.

The downswing with the sand iron, as with any other club, should be initiated by your legs (specifically your knees), which supply the drive to get the clubhead down through the sand. Move your knees laterally.

To avoid the common tendency to *scoop* — that is, to hit the ball first, rather than the sand — be sure

(A) Set the clubface in an open position on sand iron shots.

(B) Your objective is to slice a portion of sand from under *the ball to lift it.*

(C) A full backswing and follow-through are essential on all bunker shots.

to keep your eyes focused on the spot two inches behind the ball and keep your hands well ahead of the clubhead through impact. You want to feel that the clubhead is still descending even after the ball has left the sand.

The length of the follow-through, like the back-swing, should be full. Your hands must finish high to insure that you don't *quit* (stop after impact).

The two things to fear the most on bunker shots are leaving the ball in the sand and hitting it beyond the green. Leaving the ball in the sand is usually caused by hitting too far behind the ball as a result of overusing arms and hands and underusing the lower body, hips, legs, and feet. Hitting the ball over the green is caused by taking too little sand behind the ball as a result of swinging too hard, using too much right hand, or focusing your eyes on the ball instead of the sand. A helpful tip for avoiding such problems: make a *complete* golf swing, both back and through.

DRY, SOFT SAND OR HARD, WET SAND

The first step when hitting out of dry, soft bunker sand is to open the face of the sand wedge in the address. If the clubface were not open it would dig deeply into the soft sand, causing the shot to come up short.

As on the basic bunker shot, use an open stance and keep your eyes focused on a spot two inches behind the ball. Place the clubhead at that spot at which the clubhead should enter the sand. Your objective is to cut a thin slice of sand from under the ball, so a full swing is again important. In soft sand you can expect the club to sweep through without obstruction, so no extra force is necessary.

It is quite common with soft sand to find the ball buried, in which case you should apply the technique outlined on pages 112–114.

Hard sand is in many cases wet sand and the technique for both situations is the same. If the lie is good, if the bunker lip isn't too high, and if you have a reasonably long carry to the flag (more than thirty feet), choose a pitching wedge instead of a sand wedge. A pitching wedge has no flange to skid or bounce off the surface of hard, wet sand, so you'll be less likely to skull the shot, a common occurrence in this situation. As on a normal pitch shot, position the ball in the center of your stance with your hands slightly ahead of it laterally, keep your stance and clubface square, and balance your weight to favor your left side.

Use a smooth, upright swing and try to pick the ball cleanly off the sand's surface. Don't hit down! If you swing properly, you can expect a low shot that bites quickly.

If the ball is partly buried, if you are faced with a high lip, or if you have a short distance to the flag, then use the sand wedge. In this case you must hit the sand, so aim at a spot two inches behind the ball. Square the clubface, to eliminate the flange and get the advantage of the leading edge's cutting power. Also, square your stance, choke up on the club, and keep your weight on your left side.

Now, make a full, smooth swing: take the club straight back along the target line, and with emphasis on good leg action hit down through the spot two inches behind the ball. The ball will come out on a low trajectory, bounce, and roll.

In most cases, a buried lie results when a high shot lands in soft sand. The ball is left sitting in a depression, half encased in sand, looking somewhat like a fried egg. Don't be alarmed: the shot really isn't as tough as it looks. It just requires a few fundamental changes and some understanding.

There are three changes to make in your address: First, rotate the grip of the club in your hands until the clubface is closed. This will eliminate the bounce effect caused when the part of the sand wedge that protrudes beneath the leading edge contacts the sand first, with a closed face, the leading edge acts like a knife and easily cuts down under the depression that surrounds the ball. Second, to encourage a steeper downswing arc, position yourself with the ball farther back in your stance than usual. Having the ball back will also set your hands farther forward, which helps you cut through the sand without stopping. Third, open your stance less than you normally would in a bunker, and position 60 percent of your weight on your left side to insure that you don't raise the clubhead at impact.

Surprisingly, very little force is required to hit from a buried lie. Having the clubface closed and the ball farther back in your stance creates a low-trajectory shot that runs like a hare being chased by the hounds. There will be no backspin because the club never actually touches the ball: it's the sand that lifts the ball into the air. Your swing should be as long and smooth as possible — not hard.

On your downswing, aim at the outer rim of the depression. Expect your follow-through to be somewhat restricted by the depth the club travels under the ball. Make a conscious effort to lead your hands as far into your follow-through as the limitations of

THE BURIED LIE

(A) On buried lies, set the clubface slightly closed and on the downswing aim for the spot where you want to hit down into the sand.

(B) A stance slightly less open than for a normal bunker shot is needed.

(C) A closed clubface will give you the cutting power to get under the ball. The sand will lift the ball out.

A

B

C

the lie allow. Remember: you need a full swing, not a hard swing, to play this shot successfully.

The Very Short Sand Shot

There are two ways of playing a short bunker shot, where the pin is close to you. The first method is to *cut* the ball out — play a lob shot that stops quickly: Set the clubface wide open in the address. Then, make a short, soft, upright swing and skim through the sand two inches behind the ball. You can expect the ball to stop dead owing to a massive amount of backspin imparted by the shallow cut.

The alternative method is to open the clubface and use a full swing, but this time take a lot of sand underneath the ball. By taking more sand you slow the clubhead speed down, which guarantees that you don't hit the ball too far.

The short swing is best used for fast greens, where you don't want the ball to roll too much. The full swing serves best for a slow green or a slight uphill situation, where you want the ball to roll.

However, I should caution you that the short swing is dangerous in a pressure situation for anyone but a well-practiced bunker artist. If you lack confidence and swing too short, the clubhead and the ball might get stuck in the sand. When you swing fully you can be confident that at least the ball will get out.

(A) On short sand shots, align yourself in an open position in relation to the flag.

(B) To stop the ball quickly, set the clubface wide open and try to skim through the sand.

(C) Using the short-swing method, make a smooth, upright swing and try to cut the ball out.

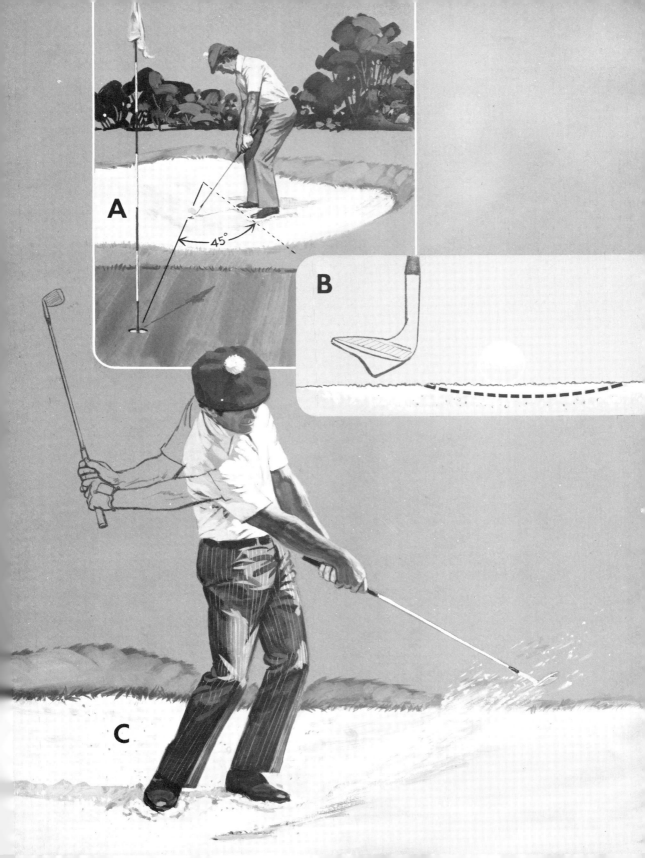

A

45°

B

C

A

B

C

Ball Buried under the Front Lip

(A) When hitting a ball buried under a bunker lip, set your feet slightly open, and be sure they are solidly planted.

(B) Aim to hit down into a spot three inches behind the ball.

(C) With the clubface square you'll have the cutting power to dig down beneath the ball. The angled clubface hitting the slope will force the sand to lift the ball out of the bunker.

First, when facing a bunker shot, you must be realistic. If the ball is directly under the front lip or really buried, you have no chance of getting out, so take a drop and a penalty. This will save you strokes in the long run.

If you face a shot that's possible, build yourself a solid platform by grinding your feet down into the sand. Flex or bend your left leg as much as necessary to offset any slope. The ball must be positioned in the center of your stance.

Now here's the trick: the clubface must be square. You'll undoubtedly say "How can he tell me to square the clubface when the ball is buried under the lip?" Easy. The squared clubface will give you cutting power, to get down under the sand; the sand will lift the ball out. All you have to do is swing fully and hit down into a spot *three* inches behind the ball. But be sure to use a lot of force — hit hard — in the downswing to make up for the mass of sand that will restrict your follow-through to just after impact. And allow for the shock of impact by gripping a little firmer than usual in the address.

Ball against the Back Edge

For even the most competent golfer, a ball against the back edge of a bunker presents a dangerous situation. Not only do you have an obstruction to your swing but also, in many cases, you have a down-hill lie to contend with. The player must be realistic: regardless of whether it's a flat or downhill lie, it sometimes pays to take a penalty stroke or to wedge out sideways if the ball is too close to the lip. You must have room to hit the sand behind the ball; the danger on this shot is that you'll contact the ball first, and send it screaming across the green.

The first step, then, is to insure that you have sufficient room to hit a spot approximately two inches behind the ball. As you address the ball, keep your eyes focused on that spot. Square the clubface: set it perpendicular to the target line. Set your weight almost totally on your left side and flex your knees to help you stay down through impact.

In the takeaway and throughout the backswing you want the feeling that you're picking the clubhead straight up, because a sharp wristbreak is essential to avoid the lip. You should, prior to playing the shot, take a few practice swings outside the trap to feel how much wristbreak is needed to avoid catching the bunker lip.

In the downswing, lead your hands down ahead of the clubhead, maintaining the cocked-wrist position you established in the takeaway until after impact.

Most importantly, be sure both to hit down into the sand, following its contour, and to swing through to the target. Feel that the clubhead is still going down after impact.

When hitting from a bunker's back edge, aim for a spot two inches behind the ball. Break your wrists smoothly but sharply and make it your objective to hit down through the spot. Make the clubhead follow the contour of the sand.

Ball below Feet

In a bunker, when the ball is below your feet a
warning alarm should sound in your head: there is
danger. Because you literally have to reach for the
ball and are forced into an awkward address position, it is very easy to hit the ball rather than the

*In a bunker when the ball
is below your feet, your
swing plane will be more
upright than usual, causing
the ball to travel to the
right — so aim yourself
slightly left of target.*

sand first and send the shot out of control over the green.

Despite this danger, take the time to think out what changes must be made to cope with the situation. If you do, and then play this shot well, you'll derive sufficient satisfaction so that any momentum that might have been lost will be back on your side.

In this situation, the ball will tend to go to the right, so aim yourself slightly to the left. To help you get down under the ball, grip at the very end of the club handle, stand as close to the ball as possible, grind your feet down, and flex your knees into a crouching position. Be careful not to cause a minor landslide that would disturb the ball and cost you a penalty.

In the takeaway, break your wrists quickly. This will provide you with a steeper downswing arc. Throughout the swing keep your head steady and your eyes focused on the sand rather than the ball. A steady head, a smooth tempo, and a conscious effort to hit down through the impact area will prevent any chance of mishitting. Keep your head down and your knees fully bent until the ball has left the trap. Because of the downslope, you feel somewhat restricted. The use of your legs and wrists will enable you to play the shot successfully.

Ball above Feet

As far as technique is concerned, the ball-above-feet situation in sand is similar to the same shot on the fair-

When the ball is above your feet your swing plane will be "flatter" and the ball will travel to the left, so aim a bit toward the right.

way or near the green (see pages 181–183). Remember, the ball is going to go to the left because of its low elevation at address. Compensate for this by aiming at a secondary target farther to the right than the actual one. Pick out a tree or bush located in the background a yard or so to the right of the pin and square the clubface to face this marker. Choke up on the grip of the club and shuffle your feet down into the sand. Unless you have solid footing, you could slip and find yourself pulling away from the ball at impact, which would be disastrous.

Position the ball in the center of your stance. Flex your knees slightly and equally distribute your weight on both feet, to help maintain balance throughout the stroke.

In the takeaway and throughout the backswing the club should follow the turning of your shoulders. There is no need for a wristbreak: this would cause the clubhead to dig deeply into the sand.

In the downswing the clubhead should be aimed at a spot two inches behind the ball. I must emphasize that the use of your hips and legs on this shot is important to drive the clubhead through the sand to a full follow-through. Force on this shot is not necessary. Swing smoothly and be sure to follow-through.

The Uphill Lie in Sand

This is one of the easiest bunker shots to play because the ball rests on a launching pad — the only way it can go is up. Start by burrowing your feet down for solid footing. Next, for good balance, flex your left knee. Play the ball in the center of your stance, with your feet aimed only slightly left of your target. The face of the club should be aimed square to the target to eliminate some of the additional height that will be created by the upslope. Aim to hit a spot two inches behind the ball.

With a full swing and emphasis on hip and leg

action in the downswing, hit through the spot in the sand. Make the clubhead follow the contour of the slope — up — as much as possible. You want the feeling that you are swinging *up*, not down, through the sand. Sweep, don't dig. Expect your follow-through to be somewhat restricted.

The ball will fly much higher than usual; consequently, you will lose distance, so don't be afraid to use a lot more force to get that ball to the hole.

On the uphill lie in sand, flex your left knee. Play the ball in the center of your stance and aim at a spot two inches behind the ball. Try to hit up the slope.

In fact, try to imagine a second target beyond the pin. If you try to get the ball past the hole, you rarely will! On long shots use a stronger club than is normal (for instance, instead of a sand wedge, use a pitching wedge to hit your usual distance).

The Downhill Lie in Sand

With a downhill lie in a bunker, the main danger is that you could take too much sand behind the ball and never get the shot out or not hit the sand at all and skull the ball. The following precautions can prevent these errors.

In the address, position the ball in the center of your stance and turn the clubface open slightly. Because of the downslope, even with the clubface open, you should expect the shot to fly low, so you must allow for this and consider the bunker lip in front of you. If the front of the bunker is high, then I suggest that you choose the safest course to get the ball onto the green. In extreme cases this could mean wedging out sideways.

Be sure to get as comfortable as possible. If you feel awkward at first standing over the ball, readdress it. If you don't feel good starting out, it's unlikely that you will play a good shot.

Take aim at the spot two inches behind the ball and keep your eyes focused on it throughout the backswing and downswing. Take the club back smoothly, cocking your wrists early in the takeaway. An early wrist-cock is essential in this situation, to

On the downhill bunker lie, get as comfortable as possible. Position the ball in the center of your stance with the clubface slightly open. Aim two inches behind the ball and consciously hit down the slope.

give you a downswing arc that parallels the slope, plus a little extra height on the shot. The backswing should be as full as the limitation of the downslope allows.

On the downswing, hit down into the spot two inches behind the ball and make the clubhead follow the contour of the sand through the impact area. To help do this you should be sure to use your knees:

drive them laterally. The legs are the sole agent to keep the club driving *low*. Even when the ball is on its way, feel that the club is still moving down the slope.

The overall swing should feel as though you're picking the club straight up and leading it straight down with your hands. Remember to allow for a low shot and for the ball to roll more than normal.

Ball Inside/Feet Outside

This bunker shot is an extreme ball-below-feet situation. The key is to adopt a posture that will enable you to hit down through the sand behind the ball.

Square the clubface to the target, grip at the very end of the handle, and bend your knees to assume an exaggerated crouching position. How much you bend your knees depends on how far the ball is below you. In some cases you may even want to kneel on your left knee and put your right leg inside the trap, or vice versa. Get into the most comfortable position that will allow you to execute the shot effectively. Balance, gained through address posture, is vital in this situation.

During the swing, be sure not to straighten your knees any more than they were at address. If you rise up, you'll hit the ball rather than the sand first. Stay down until after the ball has left the trap. Swing full, be sure to make your tempo smooth, and don't

When hitting a sand shot
from outside a bunker,
make a reasonably full
swing and be sure not to
straighten your legs any
more than they were
at address.

Choke up on the grip of the
club and get as comfortable
as possible when you're in
the bunker and the
ball isn't.

try for distance. Just try to get the ball out and onto the green.

Ball Outside/Feet Inside

This shot requires that you more or less invent a way of playing the shot. There is no set technique. Although extreme, this situation is like a normal ball-above-feet lie (the only difference is that you have to contend with the sand beneath your feet); most of the fundamentals outlined on pages 121–123 apply here.

Try various stances and select the one that feels the most comfortable. Get good footing: burrow your feet down in the sand. Grip far down the shaft. The more elevated the ball at address, the shorter you should grip the club. In some cases, this may mean you will be forced to grip the steel shaft itself.

You should remember that the ball's high elevation at impact will cause the shot to fly to the left. Allow for this when setting up. Try for the longest swing radius possible, but whatever its length, keep a smooth swing and a constant arc. And don't try for distance, but merely for improved position.

Above all, try for solid contact. It is very easy to scuff this shot. Aim to sweep the ball off the turf with a smooth motion, keeping the grip ahead of the clubhead laterally through the impact area.

The Putter Shot from Sand

Many players believe that to play anything but an explosion shot from a bunker is a cop-out. But the best shot to play is a high-percentage shot. Sometimes you'll be playing the percentages to your best advantage if you use a putter.

If the sand is firm, if the lip of the bunker is shallow, and if the ball is reasonably close to the front of the trap, your putter becomes an immediate option. However, it is not advisable to putt on soft sand, because the ball tends to burrow as it travels. Putting across a large expanse of sand, unless it is hard-packed and smooth, is also dangerous. You also have to consider these elements:

● The distance from the pin. If it is far, a putter will be difficult to gauge and control.

● The width and length of grass on the apron. Obviously, if the grass is long or the apron is wide, a putter is risky.

● The type of undulation and the speed of the green. If it's a downhill shot or a slick green, you'll be better off playing a sand wedge, because you'll get the ball to bite quickly.

If you decide to use the putter, grip far down the shaft — choke up — to insure that the putterhead remains above the sand throughout the stroke. Position the ball off your left heel. Hit slightly harder than you would normally hit a putt of the same distance on a green. Be conscious of making a smooth, well-timed stroke. Don't be in a hurry — you could top the ball and barely get out of the bunker, or worse.

Aim to hit the center of the ball as the putterhead is starting the upswing. This will produce the neces-

(A) Choose to play the putter-from-sand shot only if the lip of the bunker is shallow, as in the YES *illustration.*

(B) Try to hit just below the center of the ball as the putter head is starting the upswing. This will give you forward spin.

(C) Be sure the surface of the sand is smooth. Use your normal putting grip.

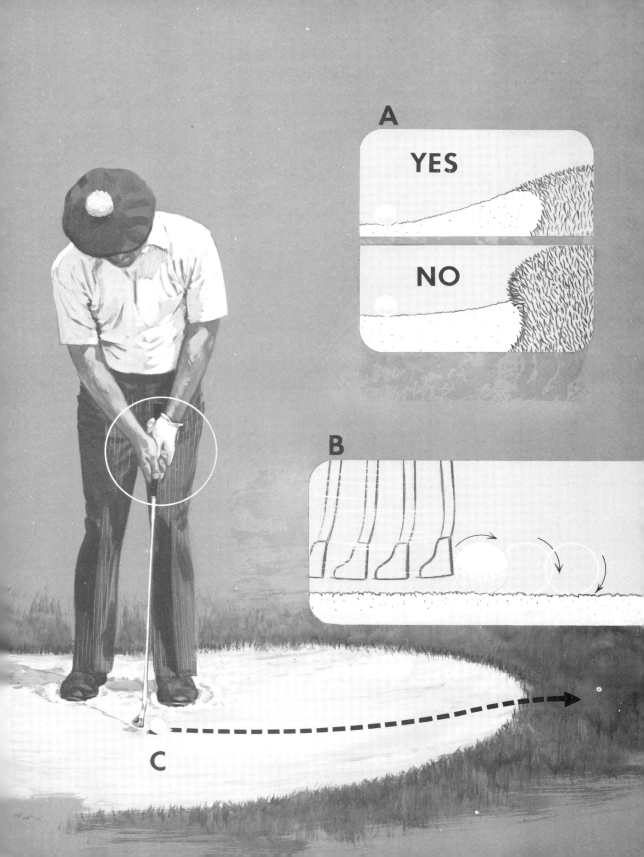

A

YES

NO

B

C

sary forward spin to assist you in negotiating any undulation. Exaggerate your follow-through to be sure that you don't stop the putterhead immediately after the ball is struck.

The Run-Up Shot from a Bunker

When the pin is all the way at the back of a long green and the lip of the trap is cut low and the ball is sitting on top of the sand, I suggest you run the ball up with a 7- or 8-iron instead of blasting out with a sand wedge. The run-up is a higher percentage shot because you will achieve a lower, easier-to-control trajectory; the long explosion shot is one of the most difficult bunker shots to play because you can never be totally sure how much sand to take. At least with a run-up the sand is not a factor: you just play the shot as if it were a normal near-the-green chip.

You need make no fancy changes: Address the ball as you would a chip shot. Position the ball in the center of your stance, choke up on the club slightly, favor the left side with your weight, and keep your hands well ahead of the clubhead laterally. The clubface should be set to face the pin squarely.

The key to the successful execution of this shot lies in hitting the ball before the sand. To accomplish this I suggest that you focus on a spot two inches in front of the ball, toward the green. This will help make you strike the sand *after* the ball.

From the start, be especially conscious of a smooth,

A

B

YES

NO

(A) When the pin is set back, the lip is low, and your lie is good, you can play a run-up shot from a trap. Simply imagine that you're playing a normal chip from grass.

(B) The YES inset shows a favorable lie; in the NO situation you would have to blast out.

well-timed stroke. Should you swing too fast or jerk the club back away from the ball, it's likely that you'll miss the shot. Keep your eyes focused throughout on that spot in front of the ball. If you don't, you will hit the sand and lose any possible overspin. You'll want to use a little wrist action in the swing also, to help you pick the ball cleanly off the surface of the sand. Keep your hands well ahead of the clubhead laterally through impact.

The Deep Trap

Average golfers often have two inclinations when they get into a deep trap near the green. They mistakenly think (1) that they need to scoop the ball up (it's almost as if they don't trust the club's loft to do the job, so they use wrists and body to try to help the ball into the air); and (2) that they need brute force to get the ball out. Actually, technique is the requisite, not brute force. Don't try for distance: let it happen as a result of the fundamental changes you make. Let the clubface do the work.

First, since you are obviously going to need a high trajectory, turn the clubface wide open. It should face the sky and be as flat as a frying pan parallel to the ground. Position the ball off your left heel and use a stance that's more open than normal. The more open your stance, the more the clubhead will cross the target line moving from the outside to the inside. This cross-cutting action, along with the wide-open clubface, will provide you with additional ball height. Also, break your wrists sharply in the takeaway. Then focus on making a *full*, upright backswing.

Taking a shallow amount of sand, attempt to simply "splash" the ball out. Make sure the clubface stays open by leading with your left hand; keep the grip end of the club ahead of the face, and don't allow the right hand to roll. Be sure to keep your eyes focused on the spot two inches behind the ball where the club enters the sand, and follow through to a full finish.

In a deep fairway trap, follow the same procedure; use a more lofted club, trust its loft, and don't try for distance.

(A) Hitting from a deep trap, an early wristbreak is essential.

(B) Set your stance wide open.

(C) The clubface should be wide open also, and as flat as a frying pan.

A

B

C

The Fairway Bunker

The swing for a fairway bunker shot should be no different from your normal fairway swing, and you should try to hit the ball, not the sand, first. For the most part, the lie determines the club you select. If the lip is low and you have a good lie, you can actually hit a fairway wood (anything from a 4-wood up); the choice is up to you. A basic change in the fundamental address is that the ball should be placed off your left heel. Use a slightly open stance and select a club that will give you the most distance. If the lie isn't too good or the lip is high, it's better to sacrifice yardage and go to a more lofted club.

As I said, the key is to hit the ball first, and for this reason, there are a few changes to make in the address. Most importantly, grind your feet down into the sand to get a solid base. If you slip while making the full swing that's needed on this shot, it could be disastrous. Choke up on the grip; this will make the low point of your swing slightly higher than usual. Place the ball in the center of your stance and rest your weight on your left side.

Now here's the real key: aim at a spot approximately one inch *in front of* the ball (laterally, toward the target). Remember: the object is to hit the ball, not the sand behind it. Keep your eyes focused on the spot ahead of the ball and try to aim the clubhead through the ball. You'll be surprised to find that the ball will be struck first, and solidly; the sand won't be touched by the clubhead until the ball is in the air.

There should be no mechanical changes in your swing. However, it is even more vital than usual to

(A) On all iron shots from a fairway bunker, choke up on the grip of the club and play the ball nearer to the center of your stance.

(B) Set your feet slightly open and place the ball off your left heel.

(C) Aim the clubhead through the ball.

(D) The lie inevitably determines what club you use. With a good lie, your 4-wood can be quite effective. Be sure to aim at a spot in front of the ball so you don't hit the sand first.

maintain a smooth tempo. Don't jerk the club back or try to hit the ball hard. Swing smoothly.

The ball will tend to fade when hit from a fairway bunker, so you should aim slightly left of your target when you align the shot. Also, use a club one gradation stronger than you would normally, because the massive amount of backspin imparted by "clean contact" will cause the ball to fly much shorter.

Ball in a Footprint

It is very hard to anticipate what the ball will do from this type of lie, so look for the easiest way out. Don't try to go for the pin or you may find yourself back in the footprint, where you started.

The key to successful execution of this shot, as on a buried lie, is the clubface position: the face must be closed. This will bring the leading edge into play and give you the cutting power necessary to dig the ball out. Assume a slightly open stance and grind your feet down to get a solid base for what will be a reasonably full swing. Position the ball in the center of your stance to give you a steeper downswing arc, and balance your weight so that 60 percent favors the left side. At the start, pick a spot in the sand approximately three inches behind the ball, and keep your eyes focused on the spot throughout the backswing and downswing.

In the takeaway, break your wrists sharply. This, and a full shoulder-turn, will give you the leverage to pull down through the sand. In the downswing, the feeling you want is that you are driving the club-head down into the footprint — literally trying to explode the ball *and the footprint* out. But be aware that, because of the closed clubface, the clubhead will dig down deeper than normal. So that you don't stop (quit) once the ball is struck, be sure to use your lower body. Effective use of the hips and knees will keep the clubhead moving through the sand. You can expect your follow-through to be somewhat restricted because of the depth the clubhead travels under the ball. The result will be a low shot that rolls a lot.

One last word of caution: if the sand is extremely gritty or hard, or if the ball is well down into the footprint, it is sometimes better to take a penalty to insure you don't get into more trouble. Remember the percentages!

Wind

Hitting against the Wind

Most players are intimidated by the wind when it's blowing against them. Instead of accepting the fact that they will lose distance, they try to hit the ball as far as they would normally by swinging harder and faster. The result is a disastrous pop-up, a slice, or a hook.

First, remember: even the 300-yard boomer has to accept the fact that distance will be lost hitting into the wind. Second: you must swing as if there is no wind at all. Think smoothness. From start to finish, don't accelerate beyond your normal calm, easy pace. Try to hit a low shot — one that will stay under the wind and give you extra roll. A high shot will always stop dead in wind and is therefore undesirable.

Position the ball between the center of your stance and you left heel, and choke up on the grip. These changes will give you a shorter, more controllable arc, as well as help insure that the ball is struck as the club is still descending, which is necessary for a low shot.

Some players have the impression that the answer to driving into the wind is to tee the ball lower. This is not the answer! If you tee the ball too low you are forced to hit down rather than sweep the ball off the tee. If you hit down too much you can easily catch the ground in front of the ball and sky the shot. Tee the ball at normal height, make the basic changes I have outlined, and try to *sweep* the ball off the tee.

Heavy emphasis must be placed on tempo. If the overall speed of your swing quickens, your right side could overpower your left, causing the clubface to arrive at the ball ahead of your hands — offering maximum rather than minimum loft to the ball, which results in a high shot. It is vital to keep your hands ahead of the clubhead through impact.

TO THE GREEN

When playing irons into the wind, you should change the ball position at address. When hitting your long irons, play the ball to the right of the normal ball position, almost at the center of your stance (see the illustration on page 170, for standard ball-position information). For middle and short irons, play the ball just to the right of center. This change will reduce the effect of the clubface loft by placing your hands farther ahead of the ball at address, thus providing you with a lower trajectory. The lower you want the ball to fly, the farther to the right you should place the ball.

At address, set your weight on your left side and keep it there throughout the swing. This will prevent you from swaying to the right, and will keep your head centered over the ball. Don't let the clubhead pass ahead of your hands laterally; you want the face to remain in a hooded position at impact. Try to finish low, with the clubhead just above waist height. This will give you a punched-type shot that has very little spin on it.

A 1-iron is an excellent club to have in your armory in windy conditions. It has only 14 degrees of loft, so using it with the fundamental changes I've just outlined produces an extra-low shot.

Hitting with the Wind

FROM THE TEE

When the wind is behind you on a tee shot, don't make the mistake that so many players do and try to knock the cover off the ball. True, the wind is going to give you a few extra yards if you execute the shot correctly, but if you make a bad swing it will also give you a few extra yards sideways. Brute force could mean the difference between being in the woods and being in the rough.

If you are looking for extra distance, tee the ball a little higher and position the ball farther forward laterally than you normally would — in other words, more opposite your left foot. Having done this, just concentrate on making a smooth, rhythmic swing. Don't jerk and don't use brute force. Just try to sweep the ball off the top of the tee, and make your overall tempo smooth.

Consider also that a 3-wood shot will often travel farther, with the wind at your back, than a driver shot; the 3-wood has more loft and gets the ball up into the maximum velocity area of the wind faster, and the higher the ball flies, the longer the wind has to push it forward.

Driving with the wind at your back, position the ball farther to the left than you normally would.

If you have a strong wind behind you when you face a shot to the green, make yourself aware of possible trouble before you select your club. Obviously, if there is a lot of trouble, such as a lake or out-of-bounds markers behind the green, then you want to be sure to select a club that will not carry the ball over. Depending on how hard the wind is blowing, this could even mean using a higher-numbered club than you would normally hit.

After selecting the conservative club, just swing normally. Don't try to slow your swing down, or you could decelerate and mishit the shot.

The Left-to-Right Crosswind

A left-to-right crosswind can be most helpful to the average player, providing it is used correctly. The most important lession in playing a crosswind: don't fight it, use it to your advantage.

For example, don't try to hit the ball straight at the target; you could find yourself in serious trouble — out-of-bounds, in the woods, or in heavy rough to the right of the green. First, visualize the shot in your mind. Take into account the wind factor as you picture the shot. Next, select a secondary target to line up with — a tree, bush, trap, or bare spot in the rough, to the left of the primary target. Then just go ahead and swing through to that secondary target. The ball will start for where you are aimed; then, when it loses spin, it will blow in toward the target. That's all there is to it. *A crosswind does not require*

TO THE GREEN

When a crosswind blows from left to right, pick a secondary target to the left of your intended target. Then try to hit the ball straight to the secondary target.

In a right-to-left crosswind, pick a secondary target to the right of your intended target. Aim to hit the ball straight to your secondary target.

any mechanical change, only an alignment adjustment.

For the player who has the ability to maneuver the ball at will, a left-to-right crosswind offers the opportunity for more distance. Simply align left and let the ball fade from left to right. The clockwise spin will be amplified by the wind, and when the ball lands it will roll twice the normal distance.

If you tend to hook the ball, you should feel comfortable in a strong left-to-right wind without compensating. Aim straight for the target. You see, the wind acts like a wall. You can't possibly hit the shot too far left, because all the hook-spin is knocked off the ball. In fact, a hook will often straighten out in this form of wind: the ball hits the wall and often seems to bounce back.

A word of caution to the player who regularly slices the ball: Since the wind will cause an exaggerated amount of clockwise spin, which will compound the results of your fault, I strongly recommend that you align yourself much farther to the left than normal.

The Right-to-Left Crosswind

In a right-to-left crosswind, align toward a secondary target at the *right* of your main objective. This secondary target could be a tree, bush, bunker, or even a spot in the rough. Once you have selected your target, after visualizing the shot and calculating how much the wind will affect it, hit toward that target.

Don't try to hit the ball straight at the main target or you might find yourself out of bounds to the left, in a bunker, in the woods, or Lord knows where. Use the wind's direction to your advantage and aim to the right. This rule, which applies if you hit the ball relatively straight, is especially applicable if you often hook sharply or make the ball draw slightly. You see, the wind in this case will accelerate counterclockwise spin on the ball and will cause the shot to curve a lot more. A fader or slicer should be a lot more at home in this kind of crosswind, because he or she can aim straight at the target without fear that the ball will land to the right. With slices, the wind acts like a wall pushing the ball back to the left.

In summary, then, assuming you usually hit straight shots, treat a crosswind like a long-breaking putt: you have to allow for the slope, or the ball will fall below the hole; you have to allow for the wind, or the ball will be blown off-target.

Water

Whoops — you've landed in the water! When you get to the ball you see that it is close to the edge of the hazard, so there is a possibility for recovery. Can you play it? Let's see.

If any part of the ball is showing above the surface, you have an excellent chance of getting it out. However, if the ball is totally submerged, even if it's just half an inch below the surface, forget it. Take a penalty and drop out.

In technique, the water shot is similar to a sand shot. Instead of blasting out of sand you will be blasting out of water, so be prepared to get wet. If you have any rain gear, put it on: it will help prevent you from worrying about getting your best golf wear wet — that fear might cause you to pull up and away from the ball at impact.

The club to select is a sand wedge, unless the ball is resting well above the water surface, in which case you could hit a pitching wedge or 9-iron. Use nothing with less loft, though. A sand wedge is ideal because of the weight, the loft, and the flange, all of which enable you to get down under the ball.

Get as comfortable as possible. Use an open stance, with the ball in the center and the clubface slightly open. Aim to hit a spot approximately one inch behind the ball. But don't touch the water as you address the ball; that would cost you a stroke penalty.

(A) A water recovery shot should only be attempted if the ball is above the surface.

(B) Even if the ball is mostly covered by water, you still have an excellent chance of recovering.

(C) If the ball is below the surface totally, forget it!

A YES

B YES

C NO

Make a full and upright backswing. In the downswing, move your knees laterally and hit down into the spot. Stay down. Whatever you do, don't pull away in an attempt to save yourself from getting wet.

Rough

Deep Rough

LONG SHOTS The critical factor in hitting long shots from deep rough is always club selection. Pick a club that has enough loft to get the ball clear of the long grass. The longer the grass, the more loft you need.

Unless you are extremely strong, the 2- and 3-irons are never a good choice — the grass creates too much resistance. Faced with a long shot, you are better off choosing a 5- or 6-iron, or a lofted fairway wood. These are percentage clubs. The fairway woods, from the 4 through the 7, are ideal. They have small heads and a sleek design, which enables you to scythe easily through the grass.

An exception to the general rule regarding club selection is wet grass. In this case you should choose a much more lofted club and just aim to get the ball back into play. If necessary, use a pitching or sand wedge. The loft and weight will give you the elevation and the cutting power essential for getting out.

The key in terms of technique is to get as little grass between the clubface and the ball as possible. To accomplish this you must start by holding the clubhead off the ground; then it won't get caught on the takeaway and throw your swing out of kilter.

An upright swing is also essential. The closer the clubhead stays to the target line (as it will with an upright swing), the more direct will be its course of attack on the ball; the clubhead will approach at a much steeper angle and will avoid the tall grass. Although you try to keep the clubhead close to the target line, a conscious effort to take the club back slightly *outside* the target line in the takeaway will help you actually do so and thus adopt an upright swing.

Because long grass has a pronounced effect on the path of the clubhead through the impact area, and on the clubface at the point of impact, there are some additional precautions that must be taken to prevent mishitting the shot. Grip the club firmly, to prevent it from spinning open as a result of the grass grabbing and twisting the head. The force of impact, regardless of how hard you grip the club, will cause the head to turn. If the face was square at address, inevitably it will be forced into an open position at impact, causing the ball to fly to the right of your target. To guard against this, close the clubface slightly at address. Then, at impact, the clubface will be forced into a square position. Even so, the overriding tendency will be to hit the shot to the right. Accordingly, you should allow for this when you align the shot.

One last, very important point: *Don't* use extra force — you don't need it. Swinging too hard is the worst mistake of all because it will make you hit well behind the ball and will only get you into more trouble. Swing smoothly!

In rough, hitting with the grain, the ball will fly lower than usual and will run when it lands.

In rough, hitting against the grain, the ball will go higher and shorter.

Hitting from a "flying lie" (when the ball is resting on tall grass, high off the ground), sweep the ball — don't dig the clubface into the rough.

Average players dread a wedge shot from deep rough around the green. They just don't know which club to use or what changes to make to get the ball onto the green. Often, through trying to hit the ball softly, they find that the clubhead gets stuck in the grass and the ball travels only a few feet. (*Caution:* be sure your grip is firm.) The sand wedge is often the best club to use in this situation. It is heavy and has sufficient loft to lift the ball over the tall grass.

Since this is just going to be a full swing in miniature, nearly all the fundamentals outlined for a long shot from deep rough apply. This time, however, instead of closing the clubface, you'll want to open it slightly. Position the ball in the center of your stance, and to compensate for the ball moving to the right, use an open stance. An upright and fairly full swing is essential. On the downswing, consciously lead the grip end of the club through to the target. Don't allow your hands or the clubhead to stop at impact. Stay down on the shot and swing through to a reasonably full finish just above waist height.

Expect the ball to roll a lot.

SHORT WEDGE SHOTS

When hitting a short wedge shot from rough, don't allow the clubhead to stop at impact. Allow for more roll than usual because of the heavy grass.

When I first showed this shot to one of my pupils he was absolutely astounded! You will be too. Who would ever consider that a putter could be an option on short shots from deep rough around the green? Surprisingly, it is a good percentage shot.

Because a putter has almost zero loft, it makes solid contact easily with a ball resting in long grass. Solid contact with a pitching or sand wedge is more chancy than with a putter, because the leading edge juts out in front of the clubface.

This shot is pure simplicity. Your object is to make

PUTTER SHOTS

(A) Take the putter up sharply with the wrists. Drop the head right onto the ball. No follow-through is needed to bounce the ball out of the rough.

(B) Only firm ground works.

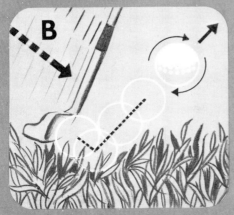

the ball bounce out of the grass! Simply align the ball in line with your right heel, and place your weight on your left side. Move your hands well ahead of the clubhead laterally. These changes, in combination with a sharp cocking of the wrists, will produce a steep downswing arc. Drop the putter-head directly onto the ball. No follow-through is necessary; just be sure to use enough force to make the ball bounce out of the rough. You can expect a high hop and a lot of roll. With practice you can learn to control this unusual shot as easily as any other. It's a great shot to have in the bag!

I caution you not to select this shot when the grass is overly wet or when the pin is less than ten feet away. Attempt it only when you have a lot of green to work with and when the ground under the grass is firm.

Shallow Rough

LONG SHOTS

The first thing to remember when hitting long shots from shallow rough is that the ball is going to travel farther than normal because two or three inches of grass will get trapped between the ball and the club-face. This prevents the grooves on the face of the club from making contact, so, instead of backspin, your shot has very little in-flight spin of any kind. This causes what is commonly called a "flier": the ball travels as though hit by a club one or two gradations stronger than the one used, and rolls a lot upon landing.

The best precaution is to select a weaker club. For example, if you think it's a 4-iron shot, use a 5-iron, et cetera. There is no need for mechanical changes in your swing. Just be aware of the extra distance the ball will fly and adjust the force within your swing accordingly.

You can choose any club you would use in a normal fairway situation. But be cautious with your club selection. Remember: take less club.

SHORT SHOTS As on a long shot, when playing a short pitch from shallow rough, you must anticipate extra roll. You won't be able to stop the ball — there will be no backspin — because grass will get caught between clubface and ball.

Select a sand wedge to give you a high trajectory, which can reduce the roll. Simply open the face of the club and your stance. Just swing normally, but allow for the ball to travel to the right because of the cutting action created by the open stance.

Above all else, remember: the ball is going to run, so swing a little easier and use less club.

Sandy Rough/Loose Impediments

Your ball has come to rest in sandy rough, or on pine needles, twigs, gravel, or cut grass. What do you do?

A

B

(A) When you address a ball that's lying on pine needles, don't ground the clubhead — that might move the ball and cost you a penalty stroke.

(B) In sandy rough, sweep the ball into the air.

Tread lightly! In moving any loose impediments from behind the ball, be careful not to disturb it; if the ball is displaced by more than half a turn, it will cost you a penalty stroke. In the same vein, don't ground the club during the address; hold the clubhead off the ground.

The objective here is to sweep the ball airborne without catching the clubhead in the impediment, so choke up on the grip of the club an inch or two. Place your weight on your left side and make an upright backswing. This will make your downswing a little steeper — so that you won't catch any debris in front of the ball. Play the ball in the center of your stance.

In the execution, be very careful not to rush the swing. It's a nerve-wracking situation, but it can be handled if you stay calm. Make your swing smooth and keep your head still and the shot will come off as planned.

6

Recovery and Challenge Shots — and How to Execute Them

Amateur's Note

In the preceding chapter, we covered many different trouble shots from the arsenal you need when you are confronted with a golf course's fundamental hazards — bunkers, the rough, water, and wind. In this chapter, we face similar challenge and recovery shots, involving other situations that you naturally consider to be troublesome too. Actually, though, they help give the game of golf its never-ending variety of man-made and natural problems to be solved (and solve them you can).

Your golf course would be dull indeed if it did not have such challenges as uphill, downhill, and side-hill lies. You would be the rarest of rare golfers if you did not at times inadvertently put yourself in a position requiring a shot that is essentially "abnormal," — an intentional hook or slice; a high shot over trees; a low shot under trees; a downhill pitch; a cut shot requiring a fast stop; a shot from a nasty lie in a divot, entailing an obstructed stance, or involving dozens of other challenges that the practice tee cannot in any way duplicate.

Do you panic? Throw up your hands and admit defeat? Never! You have the will and there is a way. Recognize the situations and heed the advice that Craig gives you in this chapter. Your enjoyment of the game will go up as your score goes down.

The Intentional Slice

Sometimes you will want to hit an intentional slice — in situations where you need to bend the ball sharply to the right around trees or other obstructions. Before you can do so, you must understand what causes the ball to slice. A slice is caused by the clubhead moving across the target line through the impact area from out to in, and by the clubface contacting the ball in an open position. The more pronounced the out-to-in swing arc, and the more open the clubface, the more the ball will slice. It's that simple.

Before the address, look toward the target from behind the ball and visualize the amount of slice you'll need on the shot. If you see the shot clearly in your own mind, you'll be able to make the necessary physical adjustments. In other words, since you obviously have to align yourself aiming well to the left of the target to allow for the slice, through visualization you'll be able to gauge the exact alignment adjustment required. Then simply pick a tree or bush as a secondary target and align your feet and body to it.

Having done this, set the clubface open (aligned square to the primary target), and at the same time, "weaken" your grip: rotate your hands to the left on the handle so that the V's formed by your index fingers and thumbs point directly to your left shoulder (this is insurance that the clubhead will return to an *open* position at impact and remain open).

KEYS FOR HITTING THE
INTENTIONAL SLICE

1. Visualize the ball in flight before your address.
2. Align toward a secondary target to the left.
3. Set the clubface square to the primary target.
4. "Weaken" your grip: point V's to your left shoulder.
5. Start the club back outside the target line.
6. Keep the clubface open by preventing your wrists from rolling.

(A) On the intentional slice, align toward, and swing through to, a secondary target well to the left of the actual target.

(B) Position the clubface slightly open, aimed at the primary target.

(C) Use a "weak" grip and be sure that your hands lead the clubhead through the impact area.

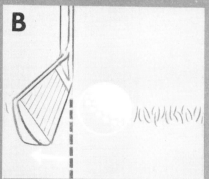

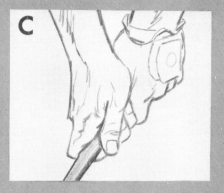

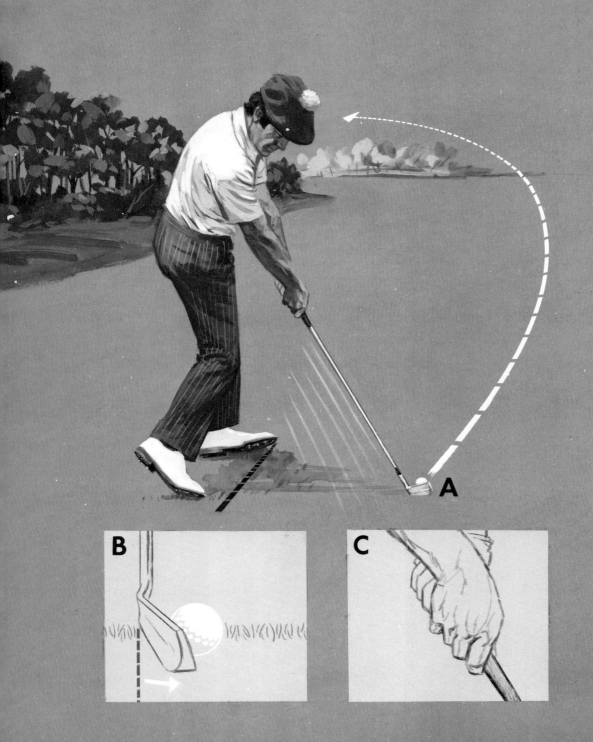

A

B

C

The Intentional Hook

KEYS FOR HITTING THE
INTENTIONAL HOOK

1. Use a strong grip:
   point V's beyond
   your right shoulder.
2. Pick a secondary
   target to the right
   of the green and
   line up toward it.
3. Close the clubface
   so it aims squarely
   toward the main
   target.
4. Hit through with
   your right side.
5. Swing smoothly.
6. Insure that your
   right hand rolls over
   your left hand.

*(A) When hooking inten-
tionally, align toward a
secondary target well
to the right of your
intended target.*

*(B) Position the clubface
closed, aimed directly at
the primary target.*

*(C) Use a "strong" grip and
make your right hand roll
over your left more than it
normally does.*

An intentional hook is a requisite in any recovery shot armory. Provided that you have a reasonably consistent golf swing, it is also an easy shot to play. There's no trick to it.

Start by "strengthening" your grip position and closing the clubface slightly. This means both V's in your grip should be rotated to point to the right of your right shoulder. This will immediately force the clubhead to follow more of an in-to-out path — a basic requirement for a hook or a draw (which has a less-pronounced curve). You'll note that after impact your right hand, because of the strong grip, will naturally tend to roll over the left more than normal, thus closing the clubface; the result will be a hook.

Your alignment determines the severity of the hook. You should pick a secondary target, a tree or bush to the right of your intended target. Once you have it chosen, close the clubface so it aims squarely toward the main target. In some cases, where you have to bend the shot around a bush or some trees, you may be unable to see the primary target, so you will have to estimate the degree of hook required and the amount the clubface should be closed. Once you have established your secondary target and have aligned your stance and clubface, simply swing normally toward that point. The ball will start off in the direction that your feet are aligned, then will hook back in. All other fundamentals — ball position, width of stance, and so forth — remain standard for the club you are using. Additional force is not necessary provided that you have applied all the fundamentals I have outlined.

Here's a special hint: To insure that your right

hand does roll over the left, I advocate making a concerted effort to drive your right shoulder under your chin. The more right-side power you apply, the more the ball will hook.

Controlling Trajectory

THE CLUBFACE AND BALL SPIN

(A) When you keep the clubface square, you get a shot with perfect backspin.

(B) When hit with an open clubface, the ball spins across the face from heel to toe, causing clockwise spin and a shot that curves to the right.

(C) If the clubface is closed, the ball spins from toe to heel, causing counterclockwise spin and a shot that curves to the left.

(D) A hooded clubface prevents the ball from gaining height; you get a low shot.

BALL POSITION AND LOFT CHANGE

By simply changing the position of the ball in your address you can change the loft on the clubface, and thus the trajectory of your shots. To hit the ball low, move the ball anywhere to the right of center. The lower you want the ball to go, the farther to the right you should play it. A standard trajectory (medium height for short and middle irons, low for long irons) will result when you play the ball in the center of your stance. A high trajectory (with short and middle irons) or a medium trajectory (with the long irons) results when the ball is positioned opposite the left heel. Playing the ball still farther to

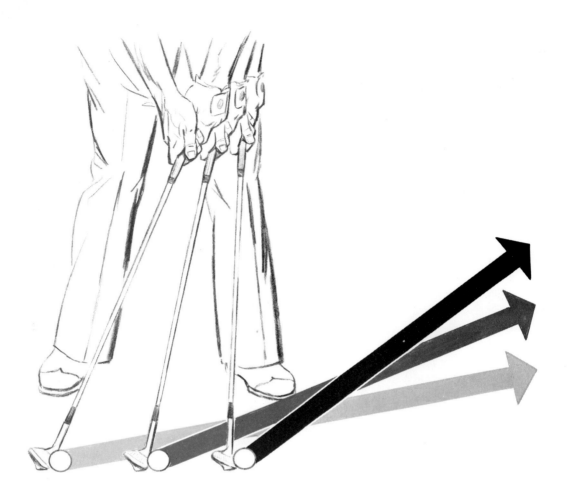

the left, with any of these clubs, will result in a still higher trajectory.

You can see from the illustration that the farther in front of the ball you set your hands, the more the loft on the face will be reduced. The more you keep your hands behind the ball, the greater the loft that will appear on the clubface. This loft principle is a simple basic that can be applied to both your address and swing.

The trajectory of the ball is directly related to its position at address. For a normal trajectory, position the ball in the center of your stance at address; play it off your right foot for a low trajectory, off your left foot for a high one.

Low Shots under Trees

KEYS FOR HITTING LOW
UNDER TREES

1. Select a driver, or
   2-, 3-, or 4-iron.
2. Choke up on the
   club.
3. Keep your weight
   on your left side
   through to finish.
4. Use a three-quarters
   swing.
5. Keep your hands
   ahead of the
   clubhead in the
   downswing.
6. Hold the grip end
   ahead of the club-
   head end through
   the impact area.
7. Finish low — waist
   high.

When you are faced with a situation that demands a low shot, such as under tree limbs, the first consideration must be club selection. This is where the 2-, 3-, and 4-irons will prove helpful. The lower the branches, the lower the club number you'll want. In some cases, where distance is required, you also have the option of using a driver. That's right, a driver! It has so little loft that the shot will invariably stay low. However, opting for a driver depends solely on the way the ball is lying. Don't use a driver to hit from a lie in heavy grass; but if the ball is lying well, or it's on hard ground, a driver is fine.

For any low shot, choke up on the grip. By gripping farther on down the shaft toward the clubhead, you'll be shortening the width of your swing arc — which will give you more control, to keep the ball down. Position the ball in the center of your stance with your hands slightly ahead of it laterally and your weight resting on your left side. Keep in mind that *your weight must remain on your left side throughout the swing.* A three-quarters swing is all that is needed.

On the downswing and into the follow-through, the clubhead must not be allowed to pass the hands. Try to lead the club's grip through the impact area ahead of the clubhead; if your hands remain ahead of the clubhead, the clubface will contact the ball in a hooded position, the loft will be reduced, and you'll hit a low shot. If the clubhead passes ahead of your hands, the clubface will return in an open position and you'll hit a high shot — just what you don't want!

A

B

C

Up and over the Trees

(A) To hit low under branches, choke up on the club's grip and position the ball in the center of your stance, with your hands slightly ahead laterally.

(B) Keep your weight on your left side throughout the swing, don't let the clubhead pass your hands through the impact area, and finish low.

(C) A driver can be very effective for a low shot if the lie is right.

Visualization plays a major part in this situation. When you are facing a shot over trees, you must first picture the shot in your mind and then base your club selection on the height and distance you have visualized. When you are close to the trees, club selection should be your major concern: be certain that you choose a club that is lofted enough. If the trees are far away, your emphasis should shift from club selection to technique. You can make any shot go higher, even with the less lofted clubs, simply by making a few basic changes. Here's how:

Set up with a slightly open stance and the clubface open too. Position the ball forward, off your left heel. Your weight should be distributed evenly between both feet. Now you are in position to make the swing.

The backswing should emphasize an upright swing. Start the club back straight along the target line. After making a full backswing-turn, unwind so that your right shoulder works it way *under* your chin. Seek the overall feeling that you are staying well behind and under the ball, not out and over it. Finish with your hands and arms high. Often, average players become intimidated by trees and, in desperation, hit down and finish low. The result, of course, is a low shot right into the tree. Sweep upward and finish high!

If you first visualize the shot — imagine it going up into the air as high as possible — then make the above changes, you'll program your muscles to give you the height you need.

To get up and over trees, use a slightly open stance, an open clubface (see inset), and play the ball farther forward than usual. Emphasis should be placed on an upright swing, and a conscious effort should be made to unwind so that the right shoulder works its way under the chin.

In thick trees or in what may seem to be an impossible situation, don't rush up and hit the ball "hoping" that you'll get out. Hustling-hitting-and-hoping will get you nowhere. Take your time and consider your options.

Try to imagine a window frame through which the ball can escape. Often, when in trouble, because of the number of trees and branches that surround you, it is possible that you won't immediately see all the openings; thus, you eliminate certain options. Only when you have considered *all* possibilities should you execute the shot. This window-frame concept will help bring *all* the openings to your attention.

Once you have spotted all the openings — windows — high or low, visualize the club that will provide the trajectory to get the ball through each. Then single out the best window; wherever possible, favor a club that you know you hit the straightest. In other words, if there is a window at 7-iron height, another of equal size at 5-iron height, and you know that you hit the 7 the straightest — you know what to select. The most important thing is to get the ball back in play safely. Remember: open a few windows to get fresh air.

The Uphill Lie

The uphill lie presents you with two problems:

First, the upslope acts like a launching pad, increasing the loft of the club and causing an extremely high trajectory; much distance will be lost to height. The ball, upon landing, is going to stop dead. To compensate you'll have to select a club one gradation stronger than normal (if you would normally hit a 5-iron, use a 4, for example). Be sure to select enough club to carry the ball to your target.

Second, you are presented with a balance problem. Your address position, because of the gravitational pull of the slope, is going to feel awkward. You must counter the tendency of having your weight forced to your right side in the address, by bending your left leg (how much you bend the leg will be determined by the degree of upslope). This will help to distribute your weight evenly between both feet, a necessity for balance.

Balance in this situation is vital. Setting your weight on your right side is asking for trouble. You'd tend to hit up on the ball too much, causing it to fly even higher and shorter than you want.

In this situation, choose window A if you are better at fading the ball than making it draw, and use a low-numbered club (for a lower trajectory) to avoid the branches. Use window B if you are better at drawing the ball, and use a more lofted club to make the ball rise quickly. The center circle is really not a "window" — it represents an almost impossible shot and the percentages would be heavily against you.

Regardless of which club you're using, position the ball in the center of your stance. Playing it any farther to the left will add even more height to the shot. And be sure that both of your knees are flexed rather than straight. The upslope has a tendency to deaden and stiffen your knees. Flexibility in the knees is vital to supply the drive in the downswing needed to hit through the ball.

In the swing, good rhythm is important. Many players who are intimidated by an uphill lie try to kill the shot — hit it too hard. This mistake most

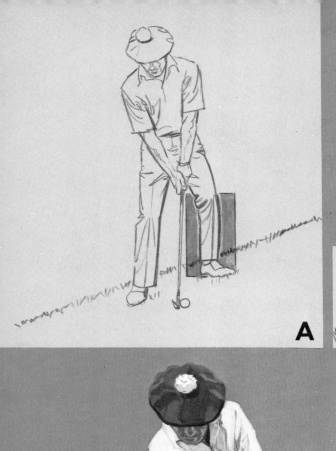

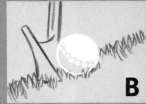

*(A) On an uphill lie, bend
your uphill leg, to offset
the slope.*

*(B) Hit a club one numerical
gradation lower than
normal (a club with
less loft).*

*(C) Try to make the
clubhead follow the contour
of the slope, and keep your
knees moving through
impact.*

often causes a snap hook. Be tempo-conscious and swing smoothly throughout.

Since balance is a problem that you must face in the swing, too, you must be sure that your weight doesn't stay on your right side on the downswing — that would cause the clubhead to be rising up toward the ball at impact. Use your knees to shift your weight to the left side in the downswing. Then, through impact and into the follow-through, try to make the clubhead follow the contour of the slope by moving your weight forward, up the hill. Avoid falling backward at all costs.

Also, allow for the ball to draw somewhat, because you'll tend to release your hands more than usual and thus will close the clubface slightly on an uphill lie.

The Downhill Lie

A downhill lie is one of the hardest shots in golf. Because of the downslope, the loft of the club you select will be greatly reduced. This causes the shot to fly lower and run farther than normal. Thus, if your position would normally call for a 5-iron to the green, you should opt to hit a 6-iron. I must add that the less-lofted clubs, such as 2- or 3-irons, are extremely difficult to get airborne in this situation, so I advocate anything from a 4-iron up.

The address is critical on downhill lies. Align yourself slightly left — place your feet in an open stance — to allow for the ball's tendency to fade. Also, to help to prevent a pulled shot (another com-

A

B

(A) On a downhill lie, set
the clubface slightly open
and put more weight on
your left side. Select a club
with more loft than is
normally required for the
same distance.

(B) On the downswing, lead
with your legs — specifically
your knees — for good
balance, and to enable the
clubhead to follow the
contour of the slope.

mon tendency), and to encourage a higher trajectory, I suggest setting the clubface slightly open in the address. The ball should be placed in the middle of your stance to make your downswing arc steeper. If the ball were played farther forward, off your left foot, the club might rise up through the impact area and you'd skull the shot.

On the backswing, because of the downslope, it becomes difficult to turn the shoulders fully. Don't fight this. A three-quarters swing will do nicely. However, try and make the plane of your swing more upright — to insure that you hit the ball, not the ground, first. Scuffing is common with a downhill lie.

On the downswing, use of the legs, specifically the knees, is essential for good balance, and it enables the clubhead to follow the contour of the slope. Emphasis should therefore be placed on a lateral movement of the knees to start the downstroke. Finally, through the impact area, be sure that the clubhead follows the contour of the slope for as long as possible.

The Sidehill Lie

BALL ABOVE FEET

With a sidehill lie, having the ball above your feet requires some fundamental changes in your address position and alignment. The most important thing to realize is that the ball is going to travel to the left. The higher the ball is above your feet, the more it will travel to the left. It's easy to understand that this kind of lie causes your swing plane to become "flatter" than normal — rather like a baseball player's near-horizontal swing. This plane causes the clubhead to leave the target line, to the left, faster than normal. The result is a hook. You can allow for the ball curving left by picking a secondary target to the right of the green. Again, how far right should be dictated by the degree to which the ball is elevated.

I cannot overstress the importance of a sound address position in this sidehill situation. I suggest choking up on the grip to offset the ball's being closer to you. Also, in this respect, I advocate standing taller — with a little less flex in your knees. These changes will help make your swing plane match the contour of the slope.

Since balance is a critical factor, be sure to place your weight toward the balls of your feet; otherwise the natural tendency could be to fall back during the swing. Finally, be very conscious of making a smooth swing. Try, as much as the limitations of the slope will allow, to swing normally.

On a sidehill lie when the ball's above your feet, stand slightly taller, choke up on the grip, and allow for the ball curving to the left by aiming at a secondary target to the right of the original target. The upslope is going to cause your swing plane to be more horizontal, which in turn will cause the ball to hook.

BALL BELOW FEET

One of the most awkward lies you can encounter is when the ball rests below your feet on a hillside. There is an ever-present danger of skulling the shot because of the awkward, restrictive stance required by the low ball position. But, with the correct fundamentals and a tight rein on your emotions, you can approach this situation with confidence.

As with other trouble shots, most of the changes called for involve the address. First, you must realize that the ball will travel to the right, because the downslope forces you to have a more upright swing plane. Allow for the ball's slice: pick a secondary target — a tree or bush to the left of the original

target — and aim toward it. How far left you set up is governed by how far the ball is below your feet; the steeper the slope, the farther left you align. There is no need consciously to hit toward your secondary target. Simply allow this to happen naturally.

The club must be gripped at the very end of the handle and your knees should be flexed more than normal. These two points will help you "get down" to the ball and hit it solidly. Also, so that you can maintain your balance throughout the swing, place your weight back on your heels.

A good point to remember is that your backswing will be somewhat restricted because of the ball position and the downslope. Don't fight this. Just take the club back to a point where you feel you can control it. A shorter, more compact backswing is desirable.

On the downswing and follow-through, be especially conscious of staying down — keep your head down (your hub steady) until the ball is long on its way. If you rise up, you might skull the shot.

(A) When the ball's below your feet on a hillside, grip the club at the very end of the shaft and flex your knees more than you do normally.

(B) Pick a secondary target to the left of your original target. The downslope will cause your swing plane to be more upright than usual, resulting in a curve to the right.

The Extreme Cut Shot

Many times you'll see a professional who's faced with a shot of some 20 to 30 yards over a really high bunker or who's playing over a bank to a tight pin placement use a sand wedge and cut the ball high into the air. When the ball lands it stops dead. This shot is rarely used by the average player.

I've shown the technique for the extreme cut shot

A

B

to many of my pupils, but for some reason they rarely practice it and are seemingly afraid to put it into use. Don't you be. This shot is an invaluable addition to your trouble-shot armory. All you have to do is practice it.

Hold the club lightly. Set your feet open. Align aiming well to the left of your intended target. The clubface should be turned wide open (as flat as a frying pan). Play the ball off your left heel. These changes alone will give you a lot more height than normal.

Make a *full* backswing-turn, taking the club straight back and up. On the downswing, try to make the swing arc parallel the foot line (an imaginary line that runs across your toes). Be conscious of leading your hands ahead of the clubhead through the impact area, and hold the clubface in the open position so that you slice under the ball. Were the clubface to overtake your hands, the face would tend to close and you'd lose the high trajectory.

Since the ball is going to fly very high, you can use a little more force than for a normal short shot of the same distance. There is very little chance — because the ball flies higher rather than longer — that you'll carry too far past the flag. Swing the club through to a full finish. In other words, you will use a full swing back and through.

One word of caution though: you should use this option only when you have a good lie. To attempt the extreme cut shot when the ball is on hard or bare ground could be disastrous. The rounded sole of the sand wedge could bounce off the earth into the ball and send it screaming over the green.

A final note: do not attempt to lift or "scoop" the ball up high. Rely on the loft of your clubhead and its downward path to do the job.

(A) A properly executed extreme cut shot will result in a high trajectory — the ball will land softly on the green.

(B) Remember to make a full swing, and try to keep the clubface open through impact.

(C) Set your feet in an open stance when you address the ball.

(D) Also, be sure to set up with the clubface wide open.

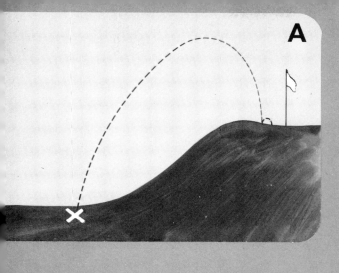

A

B

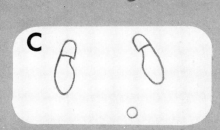

C

D

The Downhill Pitch

Whenever you are faced with a downhill, near-the-green situation, the basic rule is: use a lofted club. The steeper the downslope, the more loft you need. A lofted club will give you the maximum available backspin necessary to stop the ball quickly. Since lesser-lofted clubs like the 5- and 7-irons put forward spin on the ball, they are much harder to gauge and thus harder to control on a downhill slope.

If you have a reasonable amount of green to work with and the downhill grade is not too steep, select a spot just barely on the green and try to land the ball there. If, however, the pin is cut close to the near edge, use the fringe as a cup brake — pitch the ball short of the green and let it check and roll down to the hole.

(A) In any downhill, near-the-green situation, use an extremely lofted club.

(B) Pick a spot on which to land the ball. If the pin is set close to the edge of the green, use the fringe as a brake.

A

B

Choke up on the club slightly, place your weight on your left side, position the ball in the center of your stance, and keep your hands slightly ahead of the clubhead.

On the takeaway, break your wrists early. This will give you a steeper downswing arc and will provide you with height and backspin on the shot. On the downswing, make a slight lateral move with your knees; the knees help you to adjust to the slope and to stay well down through the impact area.

With any pitch from a downhill lie, make the clubhead follow the contour of the downslope — exaggerate the feeling of keeping the clubhead low to the ground. Keep the clubhead down low, right through to the finish. To prevent a skulled shot, which too often results from this situation, a smooth swing action is necessary.

The Left-Handed, Upside-Down-Clubhead Shot

There are times when a right-handed golfer wishes that he had a left-handed club in the bag, such as when the ball comes to rest close to a wall or some other obstacle that prevents a normal right-handed stance. You may not realize it, but there *is* a left-handed club in the bag!

All you have to do is turn a right-handed club upside down, so that the toe points downward. Then just reverse your fundamentals so that you're set up as a southpaw would be. The major change, of course,

If you're right-handed but can't address the ball normally from the right side, turn the clubhead upside down, and reverse your fundamentals so that you are set up just as a southpaw would be.

On a one-handed shot, turn your back to the target, with the ball a comfortable distance from your right foot. Pick the club up sharply but smoothly, and swing the clubhead through to the target.

is in the grip: your left hand is placed below your right.

The club I suggest using is a 7-iron, because it offers the largest clubface area and a reasonable amount of loft for height and distance.

To execute the shot, I suggest keeping the swing as simple as possible. Your object should be to produce solid contact, not to try for distance. You will be surprised at how much distance you can achieve by catching the ball solidly. Next time you are on the practice tee, be sure to practice this shot. Someday it could save a match for you.

The One-Handed, Back-to-Target Shot

Your ball is close to a tree, leaving you almost without option — seemingly with no shot selection. But there is no need to take a drop and a stroke penalty. You can delve into your shot repertoire and pull out the "one-handed shot."

Turn your back to the target, with the ball a comfortable distance from your right foot. Keep your eyes focused on the ball, pick the club up sharply but smoothly, and swing the clubhead through to the target. But remember: not designed to produce distance, this shot is solely for the purpose of getting the ball back into play to avoid a penalty. So, focus primarily on making solid contact and on using the natural weight of the club to propel the ball out.

Ball against Fence

Suppose that you were in a situation where your ball had ended up almost touching a wall or fence, permitting a right-handed shot but preventing you from taking your normal address position. Instead, the only way you can stand to the ball is with your back to the target. Have you got a shot? You have!

Provided that you can fit the clubhead between the ball and the obstacle, you're in business. Simply set up with the ball placed about four inches to the outside of your left foot and address the ball with your stance as open as the limitations of the obstruction will allow. Your back then, is almost facing the target. Now here's the trick: close the clubface until it is facing directly at your target — in other words, until it is totally closed.

All you do now is make a normal swing going back and through, holding that clubface in a closed position. Amazingly, the ball will fly in the direction the clubface is aimed.

This is just one more option that you can work on, and it's certainly one that will save you strokes in the long run. Be sure to consider it!

Under Trees on Your Knees

Some situations that may arise during a round of golf require that you employ a novel method of recovery. For instance, say the ball is resting under

Hitting right-handed, up against a fence, close the clubface so that it will be aimed directly at the target, and open your stance. Take the normal backswing and keep the clubface closed throughout.

Under a tree on your knees, keep your eyes on the ball and allow for a swinging action that incorporates a very "flat" (horizontal) plane.

the overhanging limbs of a tree and you are prevented from standing. There is still a way to advance the ball toward your target without taking a penalty: just get down on your knees!

Select a 7-iron. This club is ideal because of its broad face. Obviously, there will be no way you'll be able to sole the club (to rest the bottom of the club on the ground), so don't fight this. Once you are on your knees, try to get as comfortable as possible. Choking up on the grip of the club will help accomplish this.

Since solid contact is your primary objective, you must be very, very conscious of keeping your head still and your eyes directly on the ball. If your eyes remain on the ball throughout the backswing and downswing, you should not have any problem making solid contact. Before you start the swing, remember that you are not about to try for distance. Focus on smoothness. Because you're on your knees your swing plane is going to be very flat, so don't be alarmed when the club goes back sharply to the inside on the backswing.

Your main thought as you go into the downswing is to lead your hands in a way that will allow you to sweep the ball off the ground. Keep your hands leading the clubhead through to a follow-through position just above waist height. If you hit down, the club might get stuck and the ball will go nowhere.

Ball in a Divot

Many times you will hit a long, straight tee shot down the middle of the fairway only to find that the ball has come to rest in someone's unreplaced divot. Don't get upset — the shot is not as hard as you think. Consider that it was a club that made the divot in the first place and also that the dirt that the ball sits on is usually soft. This makes it easy for you to dig the ball out.

Unless the ball is in an exceptionally deep mark, requiring a lofted club, you can hit a fairway wood when you have a fair distance to your target. The 4- and 5-woods are ideal in this situation, because they have contoured soles *and* the loft necessary to get the ball up into the air quickly.

There should be no change in your address position. Address the ball as you would on any normal fairway shot. In the swing, though, you must be more upright — start the club back away from the ball slightly outside the target line. This will give you a more upright backswing and a steeper downswing arc, to cut the ball out. Also, on the downswing, be very conscious of making a strong lateral drive with your legs. This will keep the clubhead moving down and through to the target after impact. A hand/arm swing, with no leg action, is useless.

A mental image that I have used with considerable success is that I'm trying to make a divot within the divot. This makes me stay down and prevents me from mishitting the shot. The divot image is especially useful when using a lofted iron close to the green — when you *must* hit with accuracy to insure a successful result. No matter where the divot is, be

When hitting out of a divot, use a steeper downswing arc.

sure to allow for the ball's tendency to fly to the right by compensating when you set up.

The "Bump and Run"

You watched in disgust as your tee or second shot bounced on the back of the green and rolled over down a steep embankment. Now you are left with a shot back to a tight pin placement on a green that slopes from back to front. You realize that to select a sand wedge and to attempt to loft the ball softly to the top of the bank is risky: the ball might catch the top of the slope and roll back down to your feet, or, if you land on the green, it will roll all the way to the front, leaving you a long putt. There is only one other option: the "bump and run." Simply pick a spot on the hill and bounce the ball onto the green!

Select a club with very little loft. A 5- or 7-iron is perfect. Anything more lofted will produce too much height on the shot, causing you to miss the slope completely and fly over the green.

Hood the face of the club by moving your hands well ahead of the ball laterally. Play the ball in the center of your stance. Set your weight on the left side. Having your weight on the left and your hands well ahead of the ball will help give you the low trajectory you need.

Aim for a spot halfway up the bank. Now make a smooth half-swing. Be sure that as you swing through, your hands stay well ahead of the clubhead; then the clubhead will return to the ball with the face still in

(A) The objective on a "bump and run" is a low trajectory with limited roll.

(B) Pick a spot halfway up the hill and make a smooth half-swing. Be sure that as you swing through, your hands stay well ahead of the clubhead.

(C) In the address, hood the clubface by moving your hands ahead of the ball laterally.

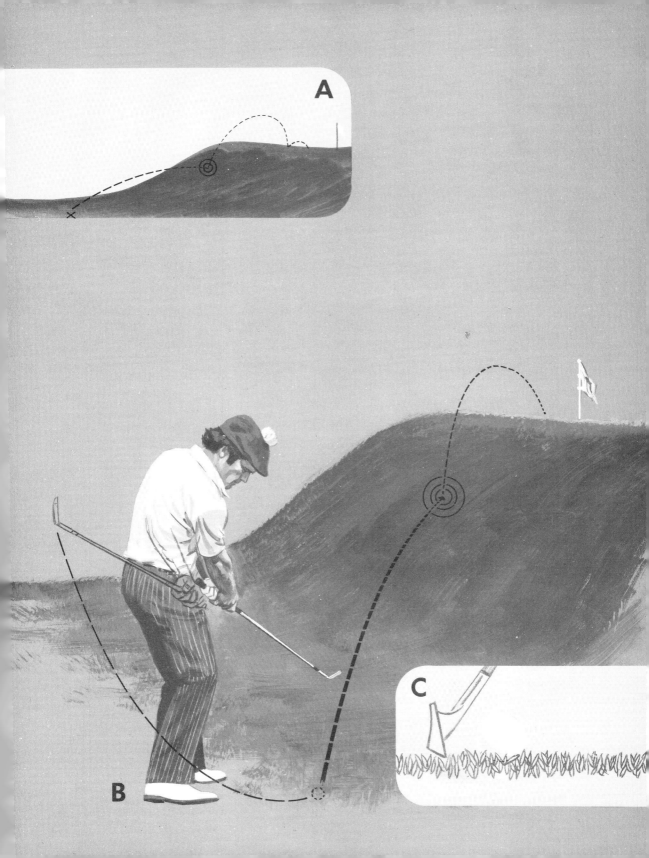

A

B

C

a hooded position, trapping the ball on the lower half of the club and preventing it from gaining too much height. Use a little more force than you would for an unobstructed shot of the same distance. You can plan on the ball hitting hard into the bank, and, because the spin is knocked off with the first bounce, it will skip softly up onto the green.

The bump and run will be less of a gamble if you try it in practice first. The simple key to remember is: "short backswing, low finish."

The Running Chip through Sand

When the pin is cut close to the edge of a trap or the overhanging limbs of a tree prevent you from pitching the ball to the flag, the shot to play is a running chip "through" the sand, if the bunker has a shallow lip and the sand isn't too soft. If the trap has either a steep lip or the sand is soft, you will have to pitch the ball onto the green in spite of the hazards or pin placement. But if the conditions are in your favor, there is an excellent chance that you can go for the flag by running through the sand, and can make an excellent recovery from what at first appeared to be a rotten situation.

Select a 5-iron. Position the ball in the center of your stance and your hands well ahead of it. This will hood the clubface to provide you with the low trajectory you need to run the ball over the sand. Choke up on the handle for control and use a light grip pressure to make sure you don't quit on the shot.

(A) To run a chip through sand, choke up on the handle and use your normal chipping technique. A nice, smooth action is needed to roll the ball across the sand.

(B) Select a 5-iron and place your hands ahead of the ball to hood the clubface.

Now use your normal chipping action, but make a conscious effort to roll your right hand over your left through the impact area. This action will cause the clubface to close at impact and impart a small amount of counterclockwise spin on the ball, which will also help it negotiate the sand. No extra force is necessary. A nice smooth action is mandatory.

The Sand Wedge to a Difficult Pin Position

The sand wedge is one of the most versatile clubs in the bag. It is effective not only for escaping from sand, but for all shots that require the ball to stop quickly, such as a shot over a water hazard or bunker to a pin placement that is cut close to the edge of the green. These are situations in which you want a great deal of height and backspin — you must toss the ball right at the flag and expect it to stop.

An exception to this height-and-backspin objective occurs when you're playing to a downhill placement, but even then the sand wedge is the ideal choice. Its 55 degrees of loft and its unique contoured sole will provide you with maximum stopping power to negotiate the downslope. Of course, you'll have to land the ball well short of the flag, but you can count on the spin to put the brakes on: the ball will roll gently down the slope to the hole. It's difficult, even hitting downhill, to roll the ball too far beyond the hole with a sand wedge — that's important to remember.

An additional advantage of the sand-wedge shot is

The sand wedge is especially effective when you have a shot over water and need to stop the ball quickly (A), when you have a short shot over a bunker and the pin is cut close to the edge of the green (B), or when you face a downhill pin placement (C). Your sand wedge provides you with maximum height and backspin.

A

B

C

that you can swing fully, both on backswing and follow-through, without fear of hitting the ball too far. On a full swing, the club's loft will give you more height, but not more distance. Thus, even the most competent of players can only hit the ball around 95 yards with a sand wedge. In playing a sand-wedge shot, be sure to focus on making a full finish. The technique is otherwise no different from the one used when hitting a pitching wedge.

7

How to Think Your Way to Better Golf

Amateur's Note

Your mind's eye, when properly used, can be an amazing stroke-saver. When improperly used, it can cause you spectacular woe.

In this final chapter, about positive thinking habits, you will see a number of references to "imitation" and "visualization," which both relate to your mental approach to golf. These two functions have osmotic qualities — they seep into your unconscious; they should be used to advantage.

Imitation means simply calling upon your stored mental pictures of the good golf swings you've seen demonstrated by your pro, exhibited on TV, used in tournaments, performed by better players in your foursome, or illustrated in such books as this one.

Visualization is something that you — and only you — can control for yourself. "See the shot before you hit it," Craig advises, "but be sure to see it as a good shot, not a poor one."

As you have perhaps discovered, your muscles will often follow the bidding of your mind, even though you are not conscious of the connection. If your out-look is negative, it has a capacity for creating rampant disaster for your golf, and with unbelievable speed. If, a split second before you swing, you visualize a shot mishit into the bunker (surely buried), then shudder at the thought of missing one or more shots from the sand, and expect with certainty to follow with a three-putt green, that's probably what will happen. Why not visualize positively? As you line up that shot with the bunker between you and the flag, see the ball sailing high and true to nestle near the pin with an excellent chance for a one-putt.

Shakespeare said it perfectly: "There is nothing

either good or bad, but thinking makes it so." It's not really such a long way from the drama of the Elizabethan stage to the pound-bet drama you face on the eighteenth hole — that challenging 9-iron shot over a yawning trap between you and the flag: the result, good or bad, is usually governed by your thoughts.

Which choice will your mind's eye take? Think about it.

Mind over Matter

There are basically two requisites for developing a sound golf game: (1) the physical aspect — sound basics and a fundamentally correct swing, and (2) the mental process — the ability to program your mind for positive action.

Throughout this chapter I will refer to the physical aspect as the "mechanics" of the swing. The *mechanics* are the individual components that make up the swing as a whole. The *mental process* is the sum of the individual thoughts you use to refine your swing or make it work. I contend that in the past golf instructors and technicians have spent too much time focusing on the physical aspects and almost no time on the thought process. After all, it is the mental process that makes good and bad shots happen.

I have seen players with terrible-looking swings produce some of the finest shots and score some of the lowest rounds. The power of positive thought, the ability to forecast a successful result, offsets their many physical deficiencies. Conversely, I have seen players with good-looking swings hit horrendous shots. The power of negative thought, the tendency to project failure, offsets the physical attributes of their swings.

In this chapter I shall focus on the key areas of the positive thought process as they relate to your golf swing and to your thinking on the golf course. My primary purpose is to make you aware of the mental changes needed to improve both your golf swing and your scoring ability. You will be amazed and gratified at the progress you'll make if you properly program yourself.

Program Your Mind to Improve Your Swing

I am convinced that in the future teachers will give much greater emphasis to the use of visual aids and imitation than to verbal instruction when teaching their students how to swing. I have found in my own teaching that verbally outlining the mechanics of the swing often presents a distorted image of what good positioning looks and feels like. I have much more success when I make a player imitate me, or place a pupil in the correct position. There is a lesson to be learned from this: your mind relates easily to pictures and to new feelings.

Take youngsters to a cricket game and it's almost guaranteed that when they get home and throw a ball in the backyard they'll have adopted the same technique and even some of the mannerisms of the players that they watched earlier. Why? Because each child has a full-color sequence indelibly printed in his or her memory bank.

If you're a tennis player, you may have had a similar experience after watching a tournament on TV. You go out afterward to play one or two sets and serve and volley beautifully.

It's the same with golf. You go to a pro golf tournament and see the world's best players in action, then go back to your club and often play the best golf you have all year.

In each case, like the child, you are imitating the pros from pictures in your memory bank. Those pictures are so clear in your mind that they are easily transformed into physical feelings, different positions — better positions. Unfortunately, the images and feelings fade. But you can call on your powers of visualization to reinforce the images. An excellent method of so doing is to examine still photographs or movies. Have photos taken of your swing and compare them to a sequence showing a professional's swing. If, for example, you see that your backswing position is bad, simply imitate the professional at the corresponding stage of his or her swing. A full-length mirror is excellent for reinforcing images while you practice your swing. If you imitate diligently, until you have a clear mental picture and the feeling of what the good position feels like, eventually the proper swing will be etched into your subconscious.

I should add that any changes must be made with the realization that it takes time for the mind, consciously and unconsciously, to accept them. Your mind literally has to reprogram itself. Your muscles, too, must be redirected and allowed time to adjust to the new patterning.

Don't "Think Mechanics" on the Course

The mechanics of golf must be kept simple. A golf swing must be as spontaneous as crossing the street in traffic. It would be very difficult to walk freely if you were concentrating on the various joints in your legs. It's immensely difficult to swing a golf club with any freedom while consciously focusing on the various elements that make up the overall motion. You have enough problems to solve. "Overthinking" tends to make you look like an automaton — preprogrammed, yet clumsy.

Conscious thoughts about mechanics should be almost nonexistent on the course and should be kept to the bare minimum in practice — one or two thoughts at most. And if you focus on such a mechanical element, you must change the thought into a *picture* of what you are trying to accomplish. Then you must incorporate it into a clear image of the swing as a *whole*. Consciously focusing on one area of the swing, if you're not careful, can disjoint the natural movement, make your swing jerky.

Sometimes a club member will come into my pro shop after playing a bad round, desperate for help, and I'll suggest a lesson. On the way to the range all I'll hear is how badly the player was hitting the ball and how he had been trying this move and that move to recover.

When we get to the range he hits every shot very well. "Why couldn't I do that on the course?" he asks. The answer is simple: After hitting his first bad shot on the course, the player started to experiment with conscious swing changes in an attempt to find the cause. After two or three bad shots, his mind started to race. He panicked. Pretty soon his mental computer was feeding him stored information from all the lessons he had taken and from all the golf books and magazines he had read in the past. The result of this machine-gunning of the conscious mind was that his swing fell to pieces. His body couldn't handle the commands that his mind was spitting out. Instead of *trusting* his swing, he became too judgmental and *blamed* the swing.

The time for mechanical analysis is not on the course. You must trust your swing. Never go on a "physical" rampage and dissect your swing during a round — this will spell disaster. Your mind will be so preoccupied with mechanics that you will lose sight of your primary objectives: your target and swinging to it.

Project Your Target

A great percentage of bad shots stem from a lack of conscious awareness of where the target is. Too many players are so concerned with hitting the ball, with getting it airborne and striking it well, that they forget where they want the shot to go. If your mind doesn't have a clear picture of the target, it can't direct the body muscles effectively.

Before hitting the shot, mentally program a positive result. How many times have you pictured your shot veering left or right and landing in the woods — and then put it there? A positive forecast will create a positive result.

If you watch good players or professional golfers preparing to hit, you'll see that the very first thing they do is stand directly behind the ball, in line with their target. At this point they are presenting a clear image of the target to their conscious mind. If, say, it's a tee shot, then a spot in the fairway, or a bush or tree on the horizon, will be visually impressed upon the mind. During the entire address pattern (see pages 19–21 for specific information), this target will remain clearly in their mind's eye. It's the same with every shot. You must have a clear mental impression of where you are going to hit, pitch, chip, or putt the ball — otherwise you chances of success are slim.

Forecast a Successful Outcome

The next step in the positive visualization process is to project a successful outcome in your mind. At the point that you implant the target image (at the start of your address pattern, when you are standing directly behind the ball), you must also preview the shot you are about to hit. You must literally "see" in your mind a clear image of the swing and the entire shot. Picture your swing at its best (a lovely flowing motion), the complete flight pattern and trajectory of the shot, and the ball landing by the hole.

Use your visualization power creatively. For example, if the pin is tucked over on the right side, visualize a fade, the ball landing, spinning to the right, then rolling to the hole. The more positive your

In a bunker, the two greatest fears for the average player are leaving the ball in the trap or hitting it over the green. Dismiss those fears! Replace them with good, positive thoughts: visualize the swing you must make and picture the ball landing on the spot you select.

input is — the more you program optimistically — the more positive your output will be. Positive thought breeds positive action; negative thought inspires negative action.

Countless times I have seen players hit beautiful shots in practice, one after the other, as straight as an arrow. Then they stroll to the first tee and hit their drive into the woods! On the practice range there was no fear of failure. If they missed a shot, there was always another ball to take its place. On the first tee it's different. The shot *means* something. The player tenses up and sees the out-of-bounds dominating on the right, woods looming on the left, and a microscopic sliver of fairway somewhere in between. The mind starts programming the out-of-bound markers and issuing commands: "I've got to stay to the left because of the woods," or "I must stay to the right because of the out-of-bounds." Negative thoughts, negative image. Does he "think fairway"? Unfortunately, no! He sees himself fail in advance — the preview is of a shot going into the woods. And often, the vision becomes reality.

Perhaps a player faces a second shot over water in the club championship. She's played this hole all year and has had no trouble. Now the shot means something. "Got to get it over the water," she wishes. Negative thought. Splash!

There is but one way to prevent negativity: be positive. Focus intensely on your target, on your swing, and on the flight pattern of the shot before you hit. If you work hard enough on this there will be nothing else in your mind to spoil the outcome. The combined total of all this mental programming is the most important psychological by-product of all concentration.

And concentration, plus all you have learned about each shot's execution, will produce what this book has tried to help you achieve: a lower score, along with confidence and control over shots and situations you *previously* had feared or flubbed.

Are you intimidated by water hazards? The normal reaction is extreme tension. By focusing on positive aspects and picturing a successful result on the hole, you will eliminate the disastrous visions that too often invade your mind and ruin the shot.